Y0-BRM-206

Mentally Retarded Children

What Parents and Others Should Know

Mentally Retarded Children

WHAT PARENTS
AND OTHERS
SHOULD
KNOW

BY HARRIET E. BLODGETT

UNIVERSITY OF MINNESOTA
PRESS   Minneapolis

© Copyright 1971 by the University of Minnesota.
All rights reserved.
Printed in the
United States of America
at North Central Publishing Co.,
St. Paul, Minnesota.

Published in the United Kingdom and India
by the Oxford University Press, London
and Delhi, and in Canada by the Copp Clark
Publishing Co. Limited, Toronto

Library of Congress Catalog Card Number: 72-152301
ISBN 0-8166-0612-9

Third printing 1973

With thanks to
Sarah, Charlotte, and Jan,
who wanted me to write this book,
and
to the parents and children of the
Sheltering Arms
who made it possible

Acknowledgments

WRITING this book was possible only because of my association with the Sheltering Arms School. I want to express my appreciation to each of those who have played a vital part in the development of the school.

To the Board of Directors of the Sheltering Arms and to the Minneapolis Public Schools, for the imagination to develop this partnership program and for the continuing moral and financial support, interest, concern, and freedom-giving confidence placed in the program.

To all the staff members, past and present — teachers, their assistants, the building staff, secretarial staff, business staff, volunteers, students — for their never-failing interest in the children, and for the thoughtfulness, effort, and persistence which they bring each day to the meeting of needs.

To the parents of all the children we have tried to serve, for their trust in sharing with us their concerns and their desire to learn, and to the children themselves, with whom and through whom we have learned so much.

To the staff of the University of Minnesota Press, whose skills and experience have been of invaluable help.

January 1971   Harriet E. Blodgett

Contents

Mentally Retarded Children

What Parents and Others Should Know

1 INTRODUCTION

UNTIL recent years, mental retardation didn't get very much publicity. Some professional people wrote books and articles about it, mostly for other professionals and for students. Little was written for parents or for the general public. Parents had not voiced their concern effectively enough, and the public was not interested, or perhaps preferred to ignore the problem and keep it behind locked doors. Now, times have changed. Not only have reports of specialized studies multiplied in the professional journals and in scholarly books, but articles on one or another aspect of mental retardation appear frequently in the daily newspapers and popular magazines. Some of these articles are about special services for retardates, some about breakthroughs in research. Some are almost entirely factual; others stress human interest; still others are intended to stir readers to action in the community.

Increased attention to mental retardation is a welcome development. Parents, other family members, neighbors, teachers, social workers, employers, community leaders — we all should be concerned about this problem which handicaps 3 percent of the population in our country. But popular articles about retardation can be, and often are, misleading, sometimes even for those with professional training, and they may be seriously disturbing to parents and others who have personal responsibility for retarded children. It is understandable that this happens. Mental retardation is an extremely complex subject with ramifications in many professional specialties, yet journalists writing about it must work within rather severe limitations of space, must try to capture interest quickly, and must use a vocabulary that will be comprehensible to the average lay reader.

A reporter interviews a specialist. The specialist explains his work as best he can, trying to use familiar words but slipping into the professional terminology he is accustomed to. He may well go off at a tangent about some highly technical facet which interests him. The reporter, faced with the necessity of reducing pages of notes to a few paragraphs, selects a striking "angle" with which to engage the reader's attention and then tries to translate into journalistic prose what the specialist has said. Some professionals are adept at explaining clearly and concisely; some reporters are skilled at asking the right questions and sensitive to shades of meaning of professional language. When either the professional or the reporter falls short in the process of communication, important qualifications may be lost, emphasis may be misplaced, details may be misinterpreted.

An article may suggest that retardation occurs when infants and young children are not provided with enough stimulation. This may be true for some retardates, and partly true for others. But when a parent reads and accepts this as a statement of fact, without qualification, he may feel a guilt that is not justified. Other articles may paint a dark picture of institutions for the retarded, with the laudable purpose of arousing the public to provide funds for improving facilities and staff, but parents with institutionalized children may well be upset. A human-interest story may depict a "miraculous cure" of a "retardate" without making clear the cause, kind, or degree of retardation, arousing false hopes among parents of children with different diagnoses. "Emotional disturbance" may be linked to mental retardation in a way that reinforces the unwillingness of a parent to accept the fact of retardation. He seizes on the idea that his child is not really retarded, but, instead, emotionally disturbed. Again, there are elements of truth in such an article, for mentally retarded children often do have other problems, including emotional disturbances. However, there is also distortion. Many times, the mental retardation came first and is at the root of the emotional problems. Treating the emotional problems, while this may make living with the child easier, will not "cure" the retardation, if this is the basic problem.

So it goes. Responsible newspapers and magazines make a conscientious effort to avoid inaccuracies. They play a very important role in focusing public attention on social problems such as mental retardation and in generating public support for needed action. Given the nature of their publications and the complexity of a subject like retardation, they probably cannot avoid the oversimplification, the half-information, the misinterpretation that at times will confuse and distress readers, especially parents, who do not have a sufficiently full background of reliable information to judge what they read wisely and critically.

It is the purpose of this book to provide at least the framework of that background. It cannot, of course, be "complete." Even as I write, new research is being done, new theories explored. What I hope to do is to set down in as nontechnical a way as I can the basic information about retardation one needs to know in order to view the individual retardate realistically. The content of the chapters to follow is based on the parent education program of the Sheltering Arms, a day school and research program for mentally retarded children in Minneapolis. Specific examples and suggestions are largely drawn from my experiences there over a period of fifteen years. Some of what follows will perhaps seem elementary or merely commonsensical, but this, in my experience, is the very kind of information often overlooked.

What is the nature of retardation? What causes it? What are the limits of learning we must accept at the various levels of retardation? What problems are likely to be related to retardation? What adjustments do families need to make when a retardate lives at home? Should retardates be institutionalized? What is the role of schools? What are the special problems of retardates in adolescence? What planning is necessary for their future?

I shall not be able to answer all these questions, or other questions that may arise, definitively, for all time and for all retardates. I shall try to indicate what we — that is, those of us who work professionally with retarded children, particularly those of us at Sheltering Arms — think the answers are in general terms. Basically, what I am trying to do is to provide information to help parents find their own answers to their own problems. It should be useful for parents to be able to compare their individual experience with our experience with many retarded children. It may be useful simply to ask some of the right questions. This is what parents themselves must do whenever they read something about mental retardation, or hear a speaker, or even chat with well-meaning relatives or neighbors. What kind of retardation is being talked about? What degree or level? What is the point of view of the writer or speaker? What is his purpose? How does what is being said apply to a specific family, with specific strengths, needs, and problems? If parents will seek out from the best sources available to them as much information as they can get about mental retardation, and then constantly ask questions such as these to put what they read and hear in proper perspective, then the problems they face, and the grief they bear, will not be needlessly increased by the imperfect functioning of the communication process, and they will be better able to help their retarded child find his place in the world.

In these pages, I shall often be addressing directly parents and professional workers, especially teachers, because they are likely to be most closely concerned with the retarded child. But other relatives, friends, and neighbors who inform themselves about the problems of retardation can provide valuable and needed support for parents. Many for whom the problem has no personal implications will better exercise their civic responsibilities in ensuring proper care for retardates and providing suitable facilities if they have a fund of knowledge on which to base decisions. This book is therefore intended for them as well.

2 DIMENSIONS OF MENTAL RETARDATION

MENTAL retardation is a multiple, rather than a single, problem. We use the term broadly to designate general intelligence which is not adequate to meet the demands of living without special help. But retardation encompasses a very wide range of subnormal ability — all the way from the person requiring total care, who can achieve independence in no ways at all, up to the person just barely below normal, who has special needs in school but is likely to fit into adult society without being too conspicuous except in times of stress. The definition of retardation varies at different age levels because the world makes different demands of people at different ages. For children, a basic element in the definition of retardation is the inability to learn at a normal rate. For adults, ability to adapt to the social demands of living is more important and more stressed. If an adult can hold a job, be reasonably self-sufficient, and stay out of trouble, no one inquires much about his IQ level.

Retardation, as a description of level of functioning, has multiple causes and multiple associated handicaps. There are motor defects, sensory handicaps, speech problems; there are also emotional and personality disturbances that we don't fully understand which are related to retardation. Multiple handi-

caps occur more frequently at the more severe levels of retardation; here the causes are most often brain damage, in-
fection, or accident of development. Many of the retarded at
the higher ability levels have come from underprivileged social and educational backgrounds and show fewer associated
defects, but they still require specialized educational care. We
shall return to the question of causation in the next chapter.

To put mental retardation in perspective, it may be helpful
to look for a moment at the way in which intelligence is dis-
tributed among the total population. This distribution may
be visualized as falling along a bell-shaped curve. About 50
percent of the people fall within the average range — at the
greatest bulge of the curve. About 25 percent fall above the
average, and about 25 percent below it. At one extreme, far-
thest from the average, are the 3 percent or so of extremely
capable, bright, gifted individuals; at the other extreme, an
about equal percentage of retarded persons. There will be
more of the mildly retarded, fewer of the moderately retarded,
fewer still — far fewer — of the severely retarded. Of the ap-
proximately 3 percent of the population commonly classified
as retarded, about 2.5 percent are mildly retarded (educable),
0.4 percent moderately retarded (trainable), and only about
0.1 percent severely or profoundly retarded.

In terms of numbers, the problem of retardation is sizable.
The President's Panel on Mental Retardation published in
1962 its report to the President, *A Proposed Program for National Action to Combat Mental Retardation*. At that time,
it was estimated that there were nearly five and a half million
people in the United States who were retarded. With the increase in population since then, this number, too, would be
increased — to about six million people. The President's Panel
indicated that at the time of its study fifteen to twenty million
people lived in families in which there was a mentally retarded person, a number that also would now be higher.

A glance at the past hundred years indicates that social attitudes toward the retarded have changed over time. In the mid-nineteenth century, efforts were aimed at cure, which inevitably failed. The resulting discouragement, as well as a multitude of other factors, produced a philosophy favoring custodial care and segregation for all retardates. This philosophy endured rather widely until the late 1940's. Then began a gradual shift in approach. At least some of the reasons can be identified.

For one thing, the world has become more complex, almost day by day, putting increasing stress on the need for education and training and the importance of upgrading everyone's skills. Society has recognized that it is essential to educate all children, to the extent that their capacities permit, and has made attempts to develop wider curricula to serve children of differing abilities. At the same time, favorable economic conditions have permitted society to support study and research on all kinds of handicapping conditions, including retardation. As noted in Chapter 1, the problem has been brought out from behind closed doors and exposed to public view. Parent associations have been influential in this process, as have social service groups. One should also note the widely publicized interest in mental retardation of highly visible and respected public officials, including the late President John F. Kennedy, and his family, and former Vice-President Hubert H. Humphrey, Mrs. Humphrey, and their family.

As a result, alternatives to segregation of retardates were explored. In contrast to the philosophy prevalent earlier in this century, now there is a fairly common assumption that retardation, if not curable, can be either prevented (by medical and social advances) or improved through education and training so that institutional placement is no longer necessary for any retardate — or at least will become unnecessary soon, when enough diagnostic, counseling, and training facilities are developed. This assumption needs careful examination. What are the facts?

Medical research on causation and treatment *is* extremely important. Thus far, however, it has contributed most significantly in a few areas of causation which are specific and very rare. It will take a long time for findings on various types of retardation to be synthesized so that a broader understanding can emerge, leading in turn to new paths of research with more general implications. We have reason to hope that eventually medical advances will make possible prevention of retardation in some cases, and better management in others, but this will take time.

We have clues to prevention related to public health practices. We know, for example, that there is a higher incidence of retardation among children whose mothers did not have adequate prenatal or obstetrical care, and in children who are born prematurely. (Ironically, in one sense medical advances have increased the problem of retardation, for now the lives of many premature babies and babies with birth defects are saved who in earlier days would have died.) We know that cultural and social deprivation at early ages may have some effect on retardation. Here further medical research will make a contribution, but equally important will be social advances, which also come slowly.

Education is of critical importance, but it can only help the retarded person to become more adequate in his functioning *within the limitations imposed by his ability*; it cannot make people "equal" in ability. All the problems faced by the public schools also affect the ability of the schools to make available to retarded children the kinds of help they need. Population distribution creates other problems. Residential schools, for example, with return home over the weekend, can effectively provide school experience, supervision, and companionship for retardates, but these schools are still few in number, usually expensive, and not equally available in all geographic locations. Although progress has been made toward fulfilling society's desire to educate all children, in the direction and to the extent possible for each, there is still a long way to go.

Community facilities other than schools have similar problems. Adequate diagnosis — medical, psychological, social, and educational — is surely essential for each retardate. This is currently available in metropolitan areas, although even there one may need to get it piecemeal; outside of big cities, diagnostic services are less likely to be available. Adequate diagnosis in itself accomplishes little unless it is combined with counseling for parents to interpret the diagnosis and to give them guidance in reaching realistic decisions, and unless it is supported by a range of facilities, in addition to special classes and schools, to suit the needs of retardates at various levels and ages. Again, these facilities are more often concentrated in the metropolitan areas and even there often fall short of meeting the needs. Such facilities should include preschool programs; various kinds of work centers, perhaps in combination with public school programs, where training, experience, placement, and continuing supervision are available; social and recreational programs; sheltered workshops to provide both training for later competitive employment and long-range or terminal employment for those not able to move into competitive jobs; and full-time institutions, for some.

Although institutionalization is not, at the present time, a favored solution, yet, in the judgment of many professional people, it will continue to be necessary for some young retardates who cannot with profit to themselves or comfort to their families remain in the community, as well as for some older retardates, at least for some periods of their lives, who cannot adapt to community living. Many of the multiply handicapped children who present severe problems of physical care cannot remain in the community for long. The community, as we now know it, cannot adequately serve those most severely retarded, those at truly sub-trainable levels, beyond the age of reliable diagnosis. This would usually mean institutional placement by age five or six. The community cannot realistically serve some retardates whose presence in the family imposes on normal family members unbearable burdens. People have different breaking points. Some families can cope with difficult problems without losing their emotional balance; others cannot. Surely it is important for society to recognize the potential loss of a normal family's contributions because of the continued burden of caring for a difficult retardate. Some retarded children, at both trainable and educable ability levels, possess a combination of behavior traits which makes them too difficult to handle in community living despite a favorable family atmosphere, attitudes, and management techniques.

For those at older ages we can rely somewhat on the criterion of "the proof of the pudding." A neglected area of research is that of the adjustment of the adult retardate, especially in the community. It is easier to study children, since they are in school, where researchers can find them; or, if they are not in school, someone knows why not and we can still usually find them. Parents are willing to cooperate with those conducting studies of handicapped children because they want the problems solved. It is much more difficult to find a good sample of adult retardates in the world at large. Consequently we don't know very much about how well-adjusted retardates get along, or the ways in which they may differ from others, of similar ability level, who cannot manage community living. We do know that institutionalization appears to be the only answer, at present, for some adult retardates who, for a variety of reasons, cannot function in the community even with close supervision. We need, therefore, to find ways to make our institutions better and more effective, to improve their programs and staffing, rather than simply to abolish them.

We come back to the multiple nature of retardation. It is not simply a matter of degree of intellectual defect, although this is highly important. We must also take into account the patterning of intellectual abilities in the retardate, which may affect progress in learning and adaptation to work; patterning of emotional reactions, which may be affected by causative factors as well as by experiences and level of ability; patterns of behavioral adjustment, again determined by both some causative factors and experience; physical health and sensory or motor handicaps; patterns of family living, important in all aspects of a child's growth and development; and patterns in a society's attitude and provision for retardates, which affect opportunity for education, recreation, employment, and social acceptance, and which broadly shape the environmental climate for all retarded individuals.

There can be no single "answer" to the problems of retardation, nor can we expect that varied solutions will come quickly or easily. This is understandably difficult for parents to accept. Parents will need to work with professional people in mutual, continuing efforts to assess retardates and their problems individually against the background of the family and the community, and in the light of the best current knowledge about retardation. It is crucial that professionals keep up with new developments in their own fields, and try to be aware of what is happening in other fields. The fields of knowledge related to retardation are many — medicine, with all its specialties, education, psychology, social work, vocational training and employment, speech therapy, physical and occupational therapy. Specialists in all of these fields will need to combine their skills and knowledge to define, explore, and — eventually, we hope — understand the multiple dimensions of mental retardation.

3 CAUSATIVE FACTORS IN MENTAL RETARDATION

THE causation of mental retardation is very complex. More than two hundred causes have been identified, yet the precise cause of any one individual's retardation can be pinpointed in only about 15 to 25 percent of the cases.

Causes can be broken down into a number of categories. One, based on when the defect began, would give us three logical groupings — prenatal, at birth, and postnatal. Pediatricians indicate that probably 90 percent of mental retardation results from prenatal causes. Some of these are fairly well understood, but many are not. One group of causes, called "inborn errors of metabolism," includes the condition of phenylketenuria, in which the infant inherits as a recessive gene an inability to digest one of the amino acids called phenylalaline. This disorder can be diagnosed within the first few weeks of a child's life, and in some states, laws have been passed to make testing of all infants compulsory so that this condition is detected. It can be treated by special diet, if the diet is started early enough in the child's life, so that damage will be minimized. If not treated, it will lead to convulsive disorders and progressive deterioration to severe retardation. This is a rare disorder, so understanding its causation doesn't immediately give us much help. In the long run, however, it may lead to better understanding of some of the other bio-chemical disorders.

Genetic factors are important among the prenatal causes. We know that if two parents are both mentally retarded, they are more likely to produce children who are mentally retarded than are parents of normal intelligence. This gets confused with the kind of retardation currently viewed as being the result of extreme sociocultural deprivation, in which the child's slowness of development and limited ability seem related to lack of stimulation and the usual opportunities for learning. Presumably, one difference would be that the truly genetic cases of retardation could be diagnosed earlier, while those who are retarded as a result of sociocultural deprivation might start out seeming more normal. The major problem in making this differentiation is that tests of ability for very young children are not as adequate for long-range prediction as tests given at later ages, so very early diagnoses based solely on tests are open to serious question. The content of the early tests, mostly involving developmental and manipulative skills preceding much use of language, is less closely related to the slightly-later-developing skills making some use of language, comprehension, and early thought processes. Another basic difficulty is that the theory of sociocultural deprivation still lacks full substantiation. It is equally tenable to suppose that many retardates who would be labeled as cases of sociocultural deprivation by proponents of this theory would be considered simply genetically low-ability people by proponents of the genetic theory. Another criticism of the sociocultural deprivation theory is that it ignores some of the things we know about the course of intellectual development. Among the final stages of mental growth are advances in capacity for abstract thinking and for using symbols. One of the arguments the sociocultural proponents use is that, as these deprived children grow older, their test scores drop. This fact could equally well be explained by the concept that they lack, and did lack from the beginning (on a constitutional rather than an environmental basis), the capacity to move intellectually into the more abstract areas. The lack simply didn't show up until tests for older ages called for a capacity that wasn't there. Obviously, we need more research on this.

Genetic factors that produce retarded children also operate in parents who are themselves of normal ability. The "wrong" combination of recessive genes can preclude normal development, although we do not always know how they operate. Recent developments in chromosome analysis can help with individual prediction problems; the whole field of genetic counseling is important and expanding. Mongolism, or Down's syndrome, is now understood to result from the presence of an extra chromosome in the infant's total complement. This has been genetically studied, and it is now possible for parents to be counseled concerning the chances of Mongolism in future offspring.

Defects in endocrine functioning, most commonly thyroid defects, can produce retardation. If the hypothyroidism is discovered in the first few months of the infant's life, treatment can be begun and sometimes, but not always, the consequent retardation can be prevented.

Blood incompatibilities, the Rh negative and Rh positive problems, and others now under study, can produce brain damage. Complete transfusions at birth may rescue some of these babies, but probably not all of them; for some, the damage may already have been done. Some virus illnesses in the pregnant woman are suspected of contributing to retardation.

Most of the prenatal physiological causes of retardation which are fairly well understood are rather rare in occurrence. Most of them are believed to produce brain damage, and many produce visible health problems — convulsions, digestive difficulties — some of which make diagnosis easier. If a woman has German measles during the first three months of pregnancy, her child is likely to have a hearing defect, heart malfunction, visual handicap, or mental retardation — often in combination. X-rays of a pregnant woman can also contribute to brain damage of the developing child. Current research will add to our knowledge of what can go wrong during the prenatal period. We do know that prenatal care is important; we know that nutrition during pregnancy is important; we know that drugs and medication during pregnancy can have unfavorable effects on the offspring. These factors, however, overlap with many other social and environmental conditions as well as with genetic factors, making the sorting-out process difficult.

Injury at birth is another cause of brain damage, although not a frequent one in locales providing good obstetrical care. Premature babies are more frequently victims of damage, but we do not know all the factors associated with prematurity. In the period immediately after birth, anoxia (lack of oxygen) can contribute to retardation. For a time, some babies having trouble breathing were placed in too high a concentration of oxygen, and we had an upswing in the incidence of blindness. This kind of blindness, "retrolental fibroplasia," was found to be related to the "overdose" of oxygen. When this relationship was discovered, and the amount of oxygen was decreased, the cases of retrolental fibroplasia dropped off to almost none.

Postnatal causes of retardation fall into three groups: acute illnesses; traumatic events; and progressive disorders which were not recognized at an early age. Encephalitis, measles, and any illness which produces a long-lasting, very high fever may be of significance. The introduction of measles vaccine offers hope that retardation stemming from this cause can be prevented. Severe head injuries (concussions) may produce brain damage. Continued severe convulsions, perhaps resulting from

18

brain damage, may themselves produce further damage and deterioration.

Other handicapping conditions may be accompanied by mental retardation, whether or not both conditions stem from the same cause. Often they do; sometimes they do not. The damage to the brain of a cerebral palsied child which gives him a motor handicap may also give him an intellectual defect. The German measles which results in a child's retardation may also produce deafness. The anoxia suffered by a newborn may make him retarded, while the treatment by oxygen for the anoxia may make him blind. There are many possible combinations.

Another handicap related to retardation is seen in the child described as having infantile autism, or being autistic. This child is characterized by the inability to form, or make use of, interpersonal relationships. He appears indifferent to people; he often does not acquire speech; when he does, he often uses it in peculiar ways. He does not learn as a normal child does; he usually appears to be functioning at a retarded level in most activities, but people often have the impression that he has capacity which, for some reason, he can't use. In behavior this child often shows characteristics in common with children known to have suffered brain damage; often he has special problems in comprehension and use of language.

Parents looking for the cause of their child's retardation will not find it in a description of all the possible causes. The way to try to identify it in the individual case is through thorough medical diagnostic study, involving not only the pediatrician but the whole array of medical specialists and specific tests. Even then it may not be found, but probably the general area of causation can be narrowed down.

Relationships observed between some causative factors and some behavioral characteristics are of interest to parents. There is a wide range of ability in children described as brain damaged or neurologically impaired, for example. Many are intellectually normal, but still have special learning problems; many others fall into the mentally retarded group. Brain-injured children who are also mentally retarded often share some traits. They are often hyperactive. As babies, they reject being cuddled; often they show disturbances of sleeping patterns. Later, many have visual-perceptual problems and have trouble learning to read. Some are slow to develop motor skills in fine coordination, even though they learned to walk at the usual age. Others are physically restless, easily distracted, "wild." Some show perseverative traits, inability to shift from one activity to another, a tendency to keep doing whatever they started doing. If such a child is painting lines on a piece of paper, he keeps on painting lines until he runs out of paper. If he is drawing a house and starts making windows, he keeps on making windows until there is no more space left. Some have obsessive interests; for example, they may be fascinated by little pieces of paper or string. In this obsessive trait, they have something in common with the children previously mentioned who are considered "autistic," many of whom are fascinated by lights, wheels, or spinning objects. Some have obsessive fears. For many hyperactive and restless children, tranquilizers and other medications have proven very helpful in school situations. If the "right" medication is found and administered in the "right" dosage for the child, often he can calm down enough to get interested in learning and make a start. Once the start is made, he may gain enough controls within himself so the medication is no longer needed. Some brain-injured children do seem, with time, to learn to compensate in some fashion for their handicap; some do settle down and make better progress with learning than would have been predicted earlier.

Once a child has lived for some years in a family, it becomes increasingly difficult to sort out which traits are native, perhaps related to the cause of his retardation, and which ones result from his experience and the ways in which he has been managed. It has been noted often that many Mongoloid children are extremely stubborn. Even the very passive Mongoloid child (who has been rare in my experience) seems able to "dig in his heels" and resist, although he may do it less conspicuously than a more active, aggressive child. It might be tempting to consider stubbornness as a characteristic of the Mongoloid child, but this is not very scientific. What has his life experience contributed to his personality? Many Mongoloids are the last-born in their families. Typically, in early childhood, their tendency to be imitative and friendly makes them appealing to people. This leads them to become mimics and "show-offs," and gets them approval and applause. With this background, it isn't strange that as they grow older they continue to be self-centered, to want to be the center of attraction, and to resort to stubborn behavior if they are somehow thwarted.

Patterns of ability show much variation and influence a child's behavior, learning, and personality development. The brain-injured child of uneven ability who functions unevenly may have more frustrating experiences than the child who always performs poorly, because sometimes he can function better than at other times, and he never knows what to expect of himself. The talkative, highly verbal child can get attention through talking; if he happens to be poorly coordinated and unable to enjoy "doing" types of activity, he may rely more and more on talking. The young child whose motor skills are closer to normal can probably enjoy life more in early years than the poorly coordinated child, because he is better able at this time to compete with others. The child whose speech is markedly defective suffers frustration from his inability to communicate. He may find ingenious ways to substitute gestures for words, but he surely will have more trouble in interpersonal relationships than his playmates and classmates who can talk clearly.

Family situations influence the development of the retarded child. A retarded child who is the oldest of the family and is surpassed by his younger brothers and sisters in all sorts of activities is in a very different situation from the retarded child who is the youngest of his family; he does not have any-one treading on his heels and probably gets a considerable amount of protective attention from his older brothers and sisters. The child whose parents seek diagnostic help, accept the verdict, and try to find the best way to meet the child's problems is in a far better position for total development than the one whose parents deny the retardation, seek no help, and accept none if it is offered. The retarded child whose family is fairly well adjusted and does not have too many other prob-lems — economic, social, or interpersonal — is in a more favor-able position for development than the one whose family has a multitude of problems.

4 TAKING THE MYSTERY OUT OF INTELLIGENCE TESTS

MENTAL retardation is defined as inadequate intelligence. But just what is intelligence? In down-to-earth terms one might say it means the ability to exercise common sense — knowing enough to come in out of the rain, being able to meet new problems and solve them. A more professional definition would refer to the capacity to think abstractly and make use of symbols. Although no one has been able to work out a precise analysis, there is agreement about certain components that somehow make up what we call intelligence: reasoning, comprehension, judgment, memory. These overlap and interact with each other and with personality and motivation.

Various tests have been developed to measure intelligence. Many people are mystified by intelligence tests, even stand in awe of them. To some, such devices seem to have almost magical properties in putting limits on where a child can go and what he can do. Consequently many parents (especially parents of retarded children) are not only curious about these tests but also fearful and resentful of them. Although the measurement of intelligence, like intelligence itself, is complex, we can take some of the mystery out of it.

Intelligence testing went through a long period of experimental development. From about 1880 to 1900, the chief result was failure. Experimenters were trying to measure such things as speed of tapping; they would give a child a pencil and see how many times he could tap it in five minutes. It turned out that this wasn't related to meaningful intelligence. Finally Alfred Binet, a French psychologist, developed a new approach to the problem of measuring intelligence. He said, in effect, "Let's find out what things most children at different ages can do, and then use these as standards to judge what we should expect of other children at those ages." Then another psychologist, L. W. Stern, refined this idea, saying, "Let's not just find out what they can do and compare it with ages; let's find a way to express the comparison in a single number." So we come to the birth of the "intelligence quotient" or IQ, which is simply a ratio arrived at by comparing a child's level of intellectual performance, expressed as mental age, with his actual age.

There is no one universally used intelligence test; nor are all intelligence tests similar in form. Some are verbal: the child being tested must use words in responding, either orally or in writing; some instead require the performance of tasks involving motor skills. Some are designed to be given to one person at a time (individual tests); others are administered to groups. Group tests are used to sort children into rough ability groupings and to identify children who may need further individual study. They are not intended to provide accurate individual diagnosis and they are not used to establish a diagnosis of mental retardation. One individual verbal test widely used with children is the Stanford-Binet Scale, which is considered one of the best predictors of success with school learning. Tests for infants and very young children include the Cattell Infant Intelligence Scale and the Bayley Scale. The Merrill Palmer Scale is a test for preschool ages which makes little demand on language skills and is for that reason useful with young retarded children who have acquired little speech. The Arthur Performance Scale, available in two forms, is useful for school-age children with speech handicaps, hearing defects, or foreign-language backgrounds. The Wechsler Scales of Intelligence are of more recent origin and are available for three age levels — there is a preschool scale, a scale for school ages, and an adult scale. In addition to these commonly used tests, there are many tests designed for narrower or more specific purposes but having, often, some value as supplementary measures of intelligence: picture vocabulary tests, visual-motor-perceptual tests, visual memory tests.

All intelligence tests are "standardized." That is, in the development of each test, all tasks were presented in exactly the same way to a large number of test subjects so that it could be determined what is the typical, the average, response of. those at any given age. Standardization usually involves thousands of test subjects, carefully selected to match what we know about the social distribution of our total population. The same procedure as in the standardizing test administrations must be followed each time the test is given thereafter if a valid comparison with the "averages" is to be possible. For example, suppose I am giving a test to a young child. His mother is sitting in the room. I might be showing the child some small objects and say to him, "Show me which one we use on our hair." If the mother then interrupts and says to the child, "Show the lady the comb," that child's response can no longer be compared with the spontaneous responses of other children.

In most intelligence tests we find a mixture of two kinds of material. The first is material that is so familiar almost everyone has been exposed to it. In a given society most children are exposed to what we call "common experience." If we happen to find a child who hasn't had this exposure, we have to take this into account in interpreting the test results, but not in administering the test. A ten-year-old child who has never been to school, who has lived in a very isolated area, and who has hardly seen a book, has not had the ordinary childhood experiences; we can't interpret his test results in the same way we do those of a child who lives in a city, has been to nursery school, and watches television. This is why at the time a test is given we usually ask about the child's background, what kind of life he has led, and where, and what experiences he has had. These facts are especially important with young children. When children go to school, they are automatically exposed to some common experiences. If children have had lacks in earlier experience, we expect that school will help make up for those lacks.

The second kind of material in intelligence tests is material that it is presumed will be entirely new to everyone taking the test. Completely new material gets harder to find with time. This is a shortcoming of some tests for young children developed thirty or so years ago, when nursery schools were far less common and children didn't have access to all the educational toys they have now. Here the "history" information helps us evaluate the use a child is making of his experience.

In testing, we assume that intelligence increases with age. Why? I suppose the reason the first person did so was that it is obvious. We all know that one-year-olds can't do the things that two-year-olds can do, and two-year-olds can't do the things that three-year-olds can do. As we check this out against measurements of children, we verify our assumption. We also assume that intelligence proceeds in development from simple to complex. One way to think of this is to visualize the young child, very simple and direct, as a tiny creek. As he grows older, a tributary feeds in and then another tributary — greater verbal skill, more language comprehension. Little by little, these streams feed into the tiny creek and it becomes a bigger stream. At the same time, it is also becoming more differentiated from other streams. As children mature, they show their special different ways of thinking and solving problems, but these still rely on general intelligence, the current of the stream.

Infant tests aren't very good for predicting later intelligence. There are, however, some traits we look for in fairly young children as indicators of intelligence. The capacity to focus attention is one. Another is the capacity to see the purpose of an object or task. A retarded twenty-month-old will pick up a toy and throw it because all he sees is this action possibility; he doesn't inspect it to discover what it can do. A normal twenty-month-old will pick up the toy, look it over, and see what it can do. Some children will look at the pieces of a puzzle. They pick up the pieces; they don't understand what to do with them, so they put them back down and smile happily, with an expression that says, "I'm done now." They didn't grasp the problem or see what was to be done. A child who is problem oriented picks up the pieces and tries a solution. If it doesn't work, he doesn't stop there; he tries the pieces a different way — it still doesn't work. So he continues trying different ways until he reaches a solution. This purposive behavior, goal orientation, and persistence are part of intelligence.

We might make a simple formboard with three pieces — a circle, a rectangle, and an oval. The pieces are taken out and the child is to put them back. A normal two-year-old can do this; a child with a 50 IQ can probably do it when he is between three and four. This task can be adapted to a slightly higher age by rotating the formboard after the pieces are removed so that the circle is in front of the oval space. It doesn't seem so difficult, does it, to see where the circle has to go? Yet this involves a problem of adaptation as well as matching the spaces. It is quite a bit harder than when the pieces are directly in front of their matching spaces.

There are more difficult form-discrimination tasks involving more shapes to be matched to spaces. One of these, with ten pieces, is useful with children from about age two and a half up to five. Both the number of mistakes the child makes and the time he takes contribute to the scoring. As we watch retarded children work with this, we find that some brain-injured children have great difficulty matching the shapes and spaces, and we expect that many of them will have trouble learning to read. If a child can't discriminate between a diamond and a square and get them in the right spaces, will he be able to tell the difference between a "b" and a "p"?

At early ages, children can respond to informational questions. We show a two-and-a-half-year-old some small objects and ask him to point to the one that we eat with or that we get dry with after a bath. The child must adapt from the size of the real object to the miniature size, and to the fact that the towel may not look precisely the same as his own bath towel. This requires some ability to generalize, to think, "Well, that isn't just like my towel but it is more like a towel than anything else." There are simpler identification items in which we ask the child to point to the object as it is named for him, rather than as it is described by function. In recognition of individual differences in rate of acquiring speech, many of these early tasks are deliberately devised to permit the young child to demonstrate knowledge without requiring verbal expression.

In the later childhood years, we are less dependent on physical and motor skills. By then, children can talk more and verbal capacities are more meaningful as predictors of school learning. What a child can do in one verbal area is related to what he can do in another verbal area. Motor skills are much more specific and do not necessarily transfer to other motor skills.

We ask six-year-olds to tell us what some words mean. Normally, a six-year-old can give meaningful definitions of words which are concrete, the names of objects familiar to him from everyday experience. He can tell us what a plate is, what a table is, what a shoe is. We ask twelve- and fourteen-year-olds to define harder, more abstract words; they can tell us what "individual" means or what "attitude" means. Vocabulary items increase in difficulty from simple and concrete (the "thing" level) to more difficult and abstract.

Comparisons are another source of test content adaptable to different levels of difficulty. We ask the young child — age six or seven — to tell us how two familiar things are the same or how they are different. The normal seven-year-old will say that a car and a train are both to ride in or both have motors. Many retarded children much older than seven simply say that they aren't the same. They have no underlying concept of "sameness" into which to fit a comparison. Later on, we ask a high school youngster to tell us the chief difference between energy and effort; he might say that energy is something you have because you have it, and effort is what you do with it. He might use more and fancier words to express the difference, but what counts is that the point is seen and expressed.

In tests, we also progress from simple to complex with comprehension questions. We ask a four-year-old, "Why do we have clothes?" and we ask a fourteen-year-old, "Why do we have laws?" Both questions involve comprehension, but at very different levels of complexity. We ask a nine-year-old to work out a simple arithmetic problem which requires him to understand the process of subtraction; we ask a fifteen-year-old an arithmetical reasoning question which is much harder. We might ask an eight-year-old to listen to a one-paragraph story and answer questions about it; the same kind of task at a higher level would involve listening to a more abstract, more difficult paragraph and then reporting the content. At the

29

higher age levels, we ask for more complex thinking: problem solving, concept formation, adapting old information to
a new situation.

With normal children, intelligence tests are helpful in setting the pace, knowing when to push harder, when to relax,
when to reward for small achievement, and when to hold out
for more achievement. They help us know how to attack problems of learning or adjustment which the child may be having,
through understanding his ability level and evaluating how it
may be related to the problem. As children move into more
differentiated learning areas at older ages, test results help
in making selections. They help select which children should
be college-bound and which should not. (We tend to overrate
college, and we shouldn't; there are many things people can
do and want to do which do not demand four years of academic instruction. This doesn't mean that training may not be
needed, but college training is not the answer for everybody.)

With retarded children, intelligence tests furnish the basic
tool we use to help us determine their over-all functioning
level, see the assets and special weaknesses, and sort out differences in their abilities so that classroom work can be adapted
for them. It is helpful to a teacher to know which child has a
perceptual problem so he can't match shapes, and which child
has a motor problem so he can't use a scissors yet. When the
teacher knows these things, she knows when to praise, when
to encourage, when to assist. If a child is doing very well in
view of his difficulties, he needs the reinforcement of reward,
not the feeling of failure and criticism.

This is not to say that intelligence is everything; it isn't.
Intelligence is a limit-setter, a framework-determiner, an out-
line-drawer. Within this framework, there are many other
factors important to the child's adjustment, his achievement,
his social compatibility, his satisfactions, and his total con-
stitution. We observe and describe some of these as interests,

cooperativeness, respect for authority, being able to get along with other people. These are not purely intellectual but partly emotional and personality characteristics. Perhaps someday we will find better ways to combine the test results which tell us about intelligence with other knowledge about what is important to people. We don't know yet how to measure motivation, emotional traits, or social adaptability. It may seem that we are downgrading these traits in importance. We aren't; it is just that we have to use the tools we have. The chief point I want to make here is that a child can use his personality traits, his emotional characteristics, and his interests only within the limitations of his total ability level, and this is essentially what intelligence tests help us to evaluate.

5 SETTING EXPECTATIONS

THE expectations a parent holds for his child must be related to the child's mental ability. Many parents would like to know more about what to expect, and when. Most of you who have a mentally retarded child have already learned to modify some standards. You do not demand of your six- or nine-year-old retarded child what you demand of your six- or nine-year-old normal child, for good reason — you have learned from experience what is possible for him. Perhaps you have also received helpful information from specialists. But this is a continuing and changing problem: you have constantly to be reassessing what it is fair to expect as your child gets older. Let us try to set some guidelines.

The degree of a child's retardation forecasts his rate of mental growth and determines within some variations his final limit. One analogy that may clarify this is to compare mental growth with different modes of transportation. A gifted child would be like a jet plane which crosses the country in a few hours. The normal, average child is like a propeller-type plane that flies not quite coast to coast and takes longer. The educable retarded child is a passenger train that stops at many towns and only runs for four hundred miles. The trainable child is more like a freight train which covers sixty miles at a very slow rate. When we talk about degrees of retardation, we are dealing with differences in speed and with differences in ultimate destination. The more severe the retardation, the earlier mental growth slows up and levels off, so that trainable children reach their final mental maturity earlier than educable children, who in turn reach their final level of mental maturity earlier than normal children.

The concept of mental age is useful in discussing the differences in speed and in ultimate destination. When we say that a child of six has a mental age of three, this means that this is the over-all, average level of mental functioning which he can demonstrate. He will do better with some things than with others; he functions over a range, not at just one point on a range. Further, the six-year-old retarded child has different interests and physical capacities and wider experience than the three-year-old. He is not like a three-year-old, *except* in his over-all mental level, and this, it must be remembered, is a very important "except."

What are the destinations, in mental age, of retarded children of different ability levels? At age six, a child with a 50 IQ will have a mental age of three; at eight, a mental age of four; at ten, a mental age of five. Everything is proceeding at just half the normal rate. At age twelve, he will have a mental age of six, but, unfortunately, at age twenty he will not have a mental age of ten because in the meantime his mental growth has been completed. At adulthood, his mental age will be about eight. A brighter child, with an IQ of about 66, develops at two-thirds of the normal rate. At six, he is mentally about four; at nine, he is mentally about six. At twelve, he is mentally about eight, and at adulthood his mental age is about ten. A child at the top of a special class group with an IQ of about 80 will develop at four-fifths of the normal rate. At adulthood, his mental age will be about twelve. Other things being equal, he will not be distinguishable from the rest of the population. He is more conspicuous as a child because school imposes special demands for learning, and he probably can't keep up with the expected pace.

A child in the trainable group with an IQ of 40 at age six will mentally be about two and a half; at nine he is about three and a half; at twelve about five. When he reaches adulthood he will be mentally about six. This isn't enough mental maturity to meet the needs and demands of adult society. It is, however, sufficient to meet the goals that we set for trainable children: self-help skills, generally good habits, socially acceptable behavior, and, with training, the ability to do simple and useful tasks in a protected situation under supervision. The trainable child may learn to recognize when it is his turn to hold the flag, but this does not forecast useful academic learning. It indicates he has learned to recognize a specific symbol and to know that it means his turn, but this does not transfer to other learning. If we consider the lowest ability level we are likely to find in school, it would be an IQ of about 30. At six, a child with a 30 IQ is mentally two years old; at nine, he is three. At twelve, he is only about four; at adulthood, he is mentally about four and a half. He won't have as many skills as the person with an IQ of 40, other things being equal.

What are the implications for school learning? By the time a child with an IQ of about 50 is sixteen, his scholastic achievement will be about the first-grade level; for a child with about an 80 IQ, about the fifth- or sixth-grade level. For the average educable child, with an IQ in the mid-60 range, the average school achievement at age fourteen is probably about third grade. In another class, a slightly different average might be found. When we consider the trainable groups, it is clear that even those close to an IQ of 50 will not go very far with academic learning. A trainable child might learn to read at the first-grade level by the time he is twelve, but this is not very useful learning. First-grade reading skill doesn't match the interests of adults or older retarded children very well. Trainable children can be taught to count by rote and to memorize some simple computations, but because of inability to transfer what they learn to other situations, they cannot make much use of this learning. Sometimes at Sheltering Arms a teacher reports that in the classroom a child has demonstrated some skill with numbers, and then, in giving the child an intelligence test, I find that he can't. Why is this? Partly it is because what he learned was so very specific to the classroom situation that it had no meaning in a different setting. Partly it is because in the classroom it is the function of the teacher to help, and many children can solve a problem if they are helped at just the right point or if a mistake is corrected at just the right point. In the intelligence test situation, the child is on his own and has to depend on what he can do by himself. We can teach specific things to the children, but they may not be able to use them, and, unfortunately, this — how to apply knowledge to a new problem — cannot always be taught.

A question that many parents ask is, "Just why is it that retarded children have such severe limitations on their learning? Why can't they be taught to be normal?" The answer is simply that brains can't be created through teaching. They are there, or to some degree not there. Retarded children are different from normal children in several ways. One is the inability, or the very limited ability, of the retarded child to use symbols or abstract ideas and concepts. This inability to understand symbols has a tremendous effect on all learning transmitted by the printed page. What are numbers? Ideas of quantity. What are letters? Ideas with meaning. What are sentences? Words strung together to convey longer meanings than single words. What is it in retarded children that makes them unable to handle these concepts? Actually, it isn't what is in them, but what is not in them. The inability or limited ability to generalize, to adapt information to solve a new problem, or to use concepts are crucial lacks. We might ask a thirteen-year-old trainable what day it is and he might respond, "January." Or we might ask what month it is and he might say, "Thursday." We see trainable children who can tell us that two plus one is three, but do not know that one plus two is three. This is an example of the inability to transfer, to generalize — the inability to appreciate meaning. It takes intelligence to handle concepts of space, time, distance, and relationship. To a greater or lesser degree, retarded children lack this ability.

The early improvement a child may show in school can involve some risks for parents. Consider a young educable child who is beginning to make progress with reading. He loves his workbook and the new words he is learning; he is very pleased with himself, and so are his parents. The parents think that he has finally started and eventually he'll catch up. This just isn't true. Learning has to progress to a certain point before it becomes visible. All the time that he is getting ready to move to another visible point, he is making progress, but it is at a slow rate; you can't see it day by day, or even week by week. Parents might think that because their child was reading a first-grade book last year, he should be reading at the second-grade level this year. Actually, he may read a first-grade book for much more than one year before he is ready to move ahead.

The same is true of trainable children in their response to language stimulation and social experience. Most parents report rapid progress in vocabulary and amount of conversation during the first months their trainable children are in school. This is encouraging, but it may make parents think that the child isn't really as retarded as the psychologist said. This is a false assumption; the rapid progress is a result of the stimulation of the new experience which allows what was already going on to become more quickly visible. It wasn't a sudden jump; it was happening all along. The child was getting ready to make his move, and the group experience brought the flower into bloom. Another flower won't bloom until the gradual process of growth permits it.

In setting expectations parents must try to avoid not only expecting too much when they are encouraged by progress but expecting too little when no progress seems visible. If a child cannot do something for himself, his parents naturally do it for him, but if they keep on doing it for him, a habit will be formed that may be difficult to break. Admittedly, it is not easy to gauge the point at which a child is ready to make an advance. How does one know that at age six Johnny will be able to hang up his jacket, when he couldn't at the age of five years, eleven months, and twenty-nine days? Schools can be helpful to parents here because teachers see the child against the background of his group, while parents see him against the background of his family — a very different point of view. Both at home and at school if a child sees that he is expected to become more independent, this helps him to do so. It will take the retarded child longer; we shall need to practice patience. There are, for instance, a number of trainables in the eleven- to fourteen-year age range who aren't yet entirely independent in managing clothing. But to set an expectation on a realistic basis, we need to see what the child can do without help. We don't have to let him become completely frustrated; we can always step in with the help, but if he doesn't try, he will not learn to become more independent. Early in our experience at Sheltering Arms, none of our children could put on their own boots. There just wasn't time enough to continue forever putting boots on for them, so we had to teach them to do it for themselves.

In the early years the expectations we set for all children, retarded or normal, center around self-care — toilet training, feeding themselves, and dressing. By the time they reach school most educable children have some self-help skills; trainable children will be farther behind.

Toilet training starts in early childhood — first taking him after the fact, gradually taking him before the fact, gradually expecting him to come to you to announce the need, then expecting him to take responsibility for himself. Upon entering school, most children have an occasional accident for all sorts of reasons; it is a new situation, or they don't remember where the bathroom is, or they are accustomed to being taken by their mothers, or they are scared. We don't need to make much fuss about accidents at this stage, for the desire to be grown-up is in the child although he still needs reminding.

It is difficult to collect accurate data about ages at which reliable toilet training has been achieved for trainable or educable retarded children, for several reasons. One is that, unless parents have been unusually careful about record-keeping, reports from memory are not very reliable, especially when there are several children in a family and what happened with one child gets confused with what happened with another. It is also true that the definition of when a child is "toilet-trained" depends partly on the parent-reporter's subjective view. Many parents believe that their child is toilet trained when the actual fact is that *they* are clock-trained. The child himself is not assuming responsibility — the parent is. Whether or not this means "toilet-trained" depends on who is defining the term.

In our experience at Sheltering Arms educable children usually are earlier to achieve independence in toileting than trainable children. Parents report, usually, that educable children have achieved reasonable self-responsibility by age four or five. Trainable children lag behind by another two or three years. Toilet accidents for new children in the school are generally at least two or three times as frequent for trainables as they are for educables. However, individual differences are great; some parents report very easy toilet training, at quite normal ages, for educable retardates; this is rarely true for trainables. We also have to keep in mind that at normal and above-normal ability levels, the age for achieving toilet training varies considerably. Physiological immaturity has some bearing, along with training methods, parental attitudes, and emotional factors.

The continuance of bed-wetting is another aspect in the whole matter of toilet training. We have found that, according to reports from parents, about one-fourth of both our trainable and educable youngsters in the eleven- to fourteen-year age range are still bed-wetters, at least occasionally, if not regularly. This raises some questions to which we have only partial answers: How much of the continued problem of bed-wetting is the result of habit? How much is it the result of parents becoming discouraged over training methods and gradually accepting this situation as "inevitable" or "just part of the child"? The fact that conditioning methods have proved so effective experimentally in "curing" bed-wetting problems suggests that both of these factors are involved.

In setting expectations for eating, parents should be careful not to worry needlessly about their child's eating habits and patterns. Eating is a good weapon for a child to use against parents, and he discovers it through your overconcern and anxiety. Young children have finicky appetites. One-year-olds are hungry; two-year-olds are never hungry; three-year-olds are hungry again. The anxious mother who worries because her two-year-old isn't hungry creates a three-year-old who won't eat and has tantrums about it, and a six-year-old whose eating patterns are thoroughly unhealthy. It doesn't have to be like that; the key is in the parents' hands. School children have often outgrown this stage but even if you think they aren't eating much, I would still advise you not to worry; when the child senses your worry, he will use it for his own purposes.

Some hints can alleviate the problems associated with eating. One is to decide what you are concerned about. Is it manners? Neatness? Nutrition? Sociability? If manners are the first concern with a retarded child, trouble is ahead. This isn't the time to stress manners. When quantity is stressed, we run a serious risk of encouraging retardates to become "fatties" if they have the slightest constitutional predisposition: since they have so few ways to gain approval, they will seize on the idea that the good eater pleases people; he's going to be big and strong and husky. What he will become is a refrigerator-raider. So you must control what is in the refrigerator. If there is nothing there that he shouldn't eat, he won't eat it — it's as simple as that. Some children are bread-and-butter fanatics and refuse to eat much else. This can happen because bread and butter are finger food; macaroni and cheese and soup are harder to eat and can get associated with more criticism. To avoid some troubles, parents should be careful what they criticize and reflect upon what their motivations are in regard to their child's eating habits.

Self-help skills in handling clothing constitute another area in which training and parent expectation are highly significant. Parents often say that their child *can* dress himself, but it takes so long that demanding that he do so is impractical. Consequently, they continue to dress him, with the result that he doesn't get enough practice to increase his own skill. The parts of the dressing process which present the major difficulties are fastening, tying, buttoning, starting zippers, and pulling on over-the-head shirts. Educable children up to the age of eight and trainables to eleven or older frequently have trouble getting shoes on the right feet. Shoes that don't have to be tied permit quicker independence than shoes that require tying. Boots large enough for shoes to slip into easily allow the child to learn to put his own boots on. Parents should remember that large enough clothing is a major facilitator of self-dressing. Little boys have trouble snapping the waistband of their pants if the pants barely go around them; they may have trouble enough even if the pants are roomy, but why make things harder than they have to be? Little girls can do more with dresses that button in front than with dresses that button in back. Buttons large in size are easier to handle than tiny buttons.

The contrast between groups of children in dressing skills is marked when we compare a beginning trainable class at Sheltering Arms with a beginning educable class, youngsters of about the same average age but separated in IQ levels (average) by about twenty points (IQ 46 for the trainables, IQ 66 for the educables). The trainable group requires roughly three times as much help from the teacher in getting on outdoor clothing as the educable group. I doubt that this is entirely a function of ability level, although this surely plays a part. I think a large share of the difference reflects training emphasis by parents. Trainable children, by and large diagnosed earlier, and with more visible handicaps, have not had the same expectations set by parents. Educable children, whose retardation probably was not recognized as early, were probably held to higher standards of self-help and consequently have achieved more independence. Differences in level of motor skills are also involved, but differences in parental attitude and expectation, and differences in practice, are clearly important. Selecting suitable clothing, easy to manage, is part of the process, but providing the child with time and opportunity to practice is equally important.

As the child grows older, he should be learning responsibility in other areas. It is important for a child to do helpful chores at home, not because it helps his parents but because it helps him. Realistically, anyone who has lived with a child knows it is harder to have the child help with something than to do it yourself. Making beds, cleaning up, vacuuming — these routine tasks can be done more quickly by an adult than by a retarded child who learns slowly, who forgets what he was doing, who leaves the rake wrong side up, trips over it, and then has to be taken to the doctor. It is harder to teach him and supervise him; yet these are the ways he learns to be more responsible. We need to help the child develop a view of himself as fulfilling a purpose in a useful, productive, co-operative, and helpful manner. Most of our retarded children will grow up to do more routine and more humble jobs than we do. It is important that they get pleasure, satisfaction, and reward out of work. The place for this to start, even before they know whether they are doing a good job, is with the approval of other people. This helps them persist long enough to develop some skill that merits praise.

Both educators and parents should avoid setting standards so high that the child can't reach them. At school, children should be given duties that will enable them to feel responsible as well as to develop sympathetic concern for each other and some awareness of when help is needed. If the goals are too high, there is no chance for reward or satisfaction; the child is deprived of motivation he might otherwise have. Expectations should be set on the basis of things he can already do so the child can be pulled up little by little. It's common for parents to want to see progress too quickly, and to be more concerned about the appearance of normalcy than with the child's genuine progress. Children should be given emotional room to grow in and should not be constantly directed in every move they make, for this overdirection puts them in an infantile situation. Because forcing a child usually stirs up resistiveness, it is best to guide gently rather than forcefully push him to achieve what is expected of him for his unique situation. In the same way, a child deserves to be treated with dignity. Never should a child's capabilities and limitations be discussed when he is in the room. We tend to overestimate what children understand when we want them to understand, and to underestimate what they understand when we don't want them to understand.

In setting expectations, we must be prepared for problems and for progress with problems, but not for the absence of problems. A child, whether or not he is retarded, should be given many chances to win praise, and should be readily praised when it is justly deserved. There are so many opportunities for punishment that it won't do any harm to overlook some of his mistakes. Although punishment is often necessary, it isn't the best way to help children learn, and should be reserved for those times when the wrong may have important consequences for the child's later behavior. Parents and educators alike must create and maintain at home and at school an atmosphere of appreciation for effort and progress on the part of the child. In so doing, it is most important to define success in relation to each child's own ability and what can realistically be expected of him.

6 HOW DO CHILDREN LEARN AND HOW CAN WE HELP THEM?

LEARNING includes a wide range of things and many different levels of difficulty. There are different ages, and stages, of learning: the infant, the young child, the school age child, the young adult — even older adults can learn. There are various kinds of learning — motor learning, memory, language, complex motor skills, reading, writing, spelling, problem-solving, invention and creativity in science, art, music. In motor learning, there is a lot of difference between the five-year-old learning to play catch in his back yard and the fifteen-year-old playing football at the high school athletic field. There are different motivations for learning and the attitude of the learner is important. There are some things you really want to learn, and therefore you're willing to make a lot of effort. There are some things you would just as soon know, but you don't really care enough to bother. There are some things you're afraid of trying.

While the level of ability determines the level of learning possible for an individual, there are other important factors that have a bearing. Emotional and experiential factors can interfere with learning. Being afraid is one — having had bad experiences and failures can make children "unready" for learning. Being distractible, or hyperactive, or unable to control attention will interfere. Being tired, hungry, lacking in physical energy, not feeling good, having a headache — all these will interfere. Having a strong desire to be doing something else when you're supposed to be learning will also interfere.

Infants, during their first several months, do 80 to 90 percent of their learning through the sense of vision. Looking around is about the only active, self-directive thing the infant can do. He can hear what is going on around him, but he may not be able to see what is producing the noise, so this doesn't teach him much. He gets fed and handled by other people, but there's not much he can do about it. He begins waving his arms and legs around, but not to any great purpose. Stimulation impinges on him, but all he can do is absorb it. He may hear something boiling over on the stove, but he doesn't know what "boiling" is, and he doesn't know what a "stove" is, so he can't learn much yet from this stimulation. As he gets a little older, he begins to handle objects — the rattles and the squeaky toys — and he begins to make sounds besides crying. Somewhat later, he can reach, grasp, and manipulate objects. The sounds he makes become syllables and sound more like speech. When he gets out of the crib and onto the floor, his world expands accordingly and he begins moving around. He's still using visual stimulation, though, to decide what to move toward. He sees the pretty crystal ashtray on the coffee table, and moves toward that. Meanwhile, his comprehension is increasing too, and when his mother says "No-no," he probably has some vague, beginning idea of what "No-no" means. He's laying some foundations for more learning.

Conditioning and habit formation are important in these early experiences. Being fed and cared for are major parts of the baby's life. At first, he doesn't know anything about the bottle until he is actually getting some milk out of it. After a time, he knows just from seeing the bottle that food is on its way.

He has made an association between seeing the bottle and expecting to be fed; these two things are now linked together like a chain. Reinforcement comes in early to help learning along. The infant's vocalizations get to be syllables, parents respond to them with approval, delight, repetition. The child is then encouraged to keep on experimenting, and the learning of language is begun. (The development of speech and language is so important for retarded children that the next chapter will be devoted to it.)

Motor learning is very closely tied to experience, practice, and maturation and readiness. More complex motor skills build on the simpler ones which preceded them. A child doesn't learn to run until after he has learned to walk. Practice is important. The beginning walker isn't very steady on his feet. His legs are short, his balance is poor, he tends to sit down suddenly with a surprised look on his face, his gait is rather lurching. But he is "set" for walking and he gets lots of practice. Soon he is an expert walker and goes on to add and refine other locomotor skills. Someone once counted the number of times an eight-year-old boy threw a ball against the side of the house in an afternoon. The count was up in the thousands. Another eight-year-old, not interested in playing ball, does something else that afternoon. He doesn't get interested in playing ball, and doesn't get better at it. Meanwhile, the first boy continues to practice, and continues to improve. A normal child can probably make a mark with a crayon when he's about a year old. It will take another two years before he can do anything as complicated as copy a circle from a model. After that, it takes about four more years before he can handle angles competently and copy a diamond.

Memory and association are part of learning. Some mentally retarded children remember specific things very well. They remember the way to grandmother's house, and if you take a wrong turn, they tell you about it. They remember that the teacher they had four years ago had a pink Ford. They may remember a volunteer who hasn't been in the building for two or three years and greet her by name. There is no question but that many retarded children do have good memory skills — for some kinds of things. There is much more question about what they can use them for. For the most part, they will remember specific, concrete, and often isolated things. The normal child remembers things, too, and he has an advantage: he hooks them together like the cars of a railroad train so that one thing leads to another. If memory exists by itself, it's like a little island, or many little islands, without a boat to get from one to another. The capacity to make associations, to hook things together, makes memory more useful. Even very young children, when they see their mother in the kitchen beginning to make dinner preparations, run to the window to start looking for their daddy's car. This is association; hooking together what's going on in the kitchen with daddy's coming home. It's partly memory, partly anticipation.

Making comparisons and differentiations is also part of learning. Even a young child may look at the piece of cake you offered him, look at the piece you gave his brother, and complain that his brother's piece is bigger. This is easier than comparisons we ask a child to make in testing when we show him a series of pictures and ask him to choose the one which is different from the others. The concept of same-different, as applied to picture materials, isn't useful much before age four to five. In more concrete comparisons, differences may be seen even though the concept development is limited.

Some learning proceeds by rote: it must be practiced over and over. And even after it is "learned," it must be used or it is forgotten. Consider spelling. Some words have to be memorized because they follow no phonetic principles at all. Children practice them, learn them, and pass their spelling test. Next week, they don't use these words, and pretty soon they have forgotten how to spell them. Whether a child gets enough continued use with something he has memorized depends partly on whether he has enough other academic skills to demand its continued use and practice. We can see this in the physical area. If you have a job that requires a lot of use of your muscles, they are probably in good shape. But if your job doesn't take much physical exertion, and you go out on Saturday and rake the lawn, your muscles remind you of it on Sunday. If you don't use your muscles, they get "rusty." If you don't use something you learned, especially if it was rote-memorized, it too gets "rusty" and is less available to you the next time you want to use it. This happens more with retarded children than with normal ones because normal children make more day-to-day use of what they learn.

Some kinds of learning proceed by trial and error. You try something, and if it works, you do it that way next time. If it doesn't work, you try something else. Some brain-injured children have a special problem in the rigidity of their patterns. They can't seem to try something different; they keep on doing the same incorrect thing over and over. Such a child picks up a piece of a puzzle, tries it, finds it doesn't fit, but can't adapt. He will continue to push and push in a repeated effort, and be unable to shift his procedure. Often, parents can be helpful here. If a child is repeating errors, keeping on with an approach that isn't going to work, try to help him vary his approach. If you can break the rigidity and help him try another method, he may be able to succeed.

Much research is going on about the learning process. One principle established by researchers that may be specially useful in working with retarded children is that learning proceeds better when a child's solution to a problem is verified quickly, when he finds out right away if he was right or wrong. This isn't a new idea, although it's good to have confirmation from research studies. We have long known that extra help in the classroom is useful partly because more individual attention permits quicker verification of answers. A fairly new application of this principle is the teaching machine, which shows the child right away if his answer is correct. If he's right, he goes on to the next problem; if he's wrong, he gets corrected before he learns his mistakes. Programmed instruction breaks learning down into tiny pieces, and this should be good for retarded children. One problem may be, however, that the retarded child is not yet sufficiently self-motivated or interested in learning. Before the retarded child can make use of a teaching machine, he will need a longer period of preparation than the normal child, in which the teacher helps to provide motivation.

Research may yield other principles and procedures that can be adapted in new devices to help the retarded child learn. In the meantime parents can help their retarded youngster by giving him experience and practice, and reward for success.

Retarded children need much experience in pre-academic learning. To see and hear differences in words and letters, to follow directions, to make use of numbers, to sit still, to acquire general information, to take something already learned and apply it in another setting — these are experiences retarded children need in abundance. They need lots of language, communication, explaining. You often don't think of explaining things to a retarded child because you assume he sees what is going on. He does, with his eyes, but he doesn't know what it means unless you tell him. What you need to do with your retarded child is very much what you do, naturally and comfortably, with your normal three-, four-, and five-year-olds; this is what retarded children continue to need much longer. This is readiness-building, and for some, learning will not go much further. But they will at least have acquired a store of information, and information puts meanings into living. Telling stories is a very good device. All young children enjoy stories about themselves and stories of all kinds which you tell them rather than read to them. As children grow older, up to the early school ages, they continue to prefer stories which are told to them rather than read to them. With retarded children, this preference is even more marked. The "told" story is more concrete, closer to the reality level, with less distance between teller and listener. Much useful information can be conveyed through stories.

When the retarded child does learn something, we should reward him with praise so that he'll be encouraged to keep on trying. If he learns to eat with a fork instead of a spoon, this is an achievement. If he learns to color inside the lines two-thirds of the time instead of one-third of the time, this is an achievement. We still need to keep this within the framework of the expectation, because it is not achievement at a normal level. It is, however, an achievement for him in which we can take real pleasure and show him our pleasure. It is important not to underrate the little gains. For example, a child learns to ride a two-wheel bicycle; his parents have been working on this for four years, and one reaction they might have, stemming from their long effort and multiple frustrations, is, "Well, it's about time!" A better one, putting the focus on the child's achievement, would be "Good! You can do it now!" Or "Isn't that great — you're riding, all by yourself!" Whenever something becomes the child's success is a good time to appreciate it. Just because it took longer than expected doesn't make it any less valuable. Part of the motivation that retarded children need to move ahead comes from recognition for having moved.

For children who can do some academic work, practice is very important. Once a child has learned to read, even a little bit, the more he reads, the better, as far as reading development is concerned. Interest and motivation are essential. Too much pressure to read can make a child hate reading; material which is too difficult can defeat him. If he can read easy material, encourage him to read more easy material; don't try to move him too quickly into more difficult material which he can't read with either accuracy or enjoyment. If he comes to words he doesn't know, tell him what they are, so that the pleasure of the story isn't lost while he struggles with a word. What you're most interested in is encouraging interest, enthusiasm, and motivation. I think it's better if you encourage him to read for fun, and increase his pleasure by your pleasure in his successes. When he can read by himself for pleasure, you can ask him to tell you about the story; this is a good way to check on his comprehension of what he is reading. But don't push too hard; don't let efforts to learn get associated with unpleasantness, impatience, failure, or unhappiness at home.

School learning, it should be reiterated, is not the most crucial element in the lives of mentally retarded children. More basic, and more important, are some of the things you can help build at home — basic self-care, self-help skills, acceptable behavior, cooperativeness, emotional control, satisfying interests. Parents are in the very best position to help a child develop these kinds of learning which are so important in determining how other people will accept him and feel about him. We often take them for granted because normal children quickly master them. But they are far from automatic in retarded children; they need to be patiently taught. What you do in helping your child learn these skills and attitudes will have far more significance for your child's life than stressing academic learning.

7 SPEECH AND LANGUAGE DEVELOPMENT

PARENTS wait eagerly for their baby to learn to talk. This is so universal an attitude among parents that all "baby books" for family record-keeping include a place to write down the first word and the circumstances under which it was said. Often it is the failure of a child to begin to speak which is the first hint to parents that he is not developing mentally as a normal child does.

Speech starts with the production of sounds. Sounds gradually become more differentiated and more precise, and finally, through imitation and learning, become words. Articulation is the production of differentiated sounds in correct patterns. Language is not only the use of differentiated words but the organizing of words in sentences to convey meaning, to communicate effectively. Speech, then, which is oral language, is a very complicated thing, involving the physical structure of the lips, teeth, tongue, palate, throat, and larynx as well as mental development and social experience.

The infant at first has just the capacity to make sounds. However, he normally hears speech from the beginning of his life. As his nervous system matures a little, and he hears more speech, the vocalizations which at first were just sounds gradually take on a syllablelike quality. We call this the "babbling" stage. The syllables are repeated, and as the child hears himself making the sounds, he imitates himself making the sounds: "ba-ba-ba-ba" and "ma-ma-ma-ma." His mother hears him saying "ma-ma-ma-ma," is pleased, repeats it, and he not only imitates himself but also imitates her. First words are very likely to be just one step beyond this stage of babbling, repeating syllables. Parents assume that "ma-ma" and "da-da" mean "mamma" and "daddy." Their pleasure is communicated to the child, and the meanings get built in. At first, a child's words are only rough approximations of "real" words, but through the emotional rewards of other people's reactions, and through imitation, practice, and repetition, the child comes closer and closer to forming words clearly.

Language takes on an increasingly complex structure with growth in age and maturity. (It should be noted that all studies of language development show more rapid progress by girls than by boys.) The one-word sentence of the fifteen-month-old — "Milk" — becomes the two-word sentence of the two-year-old — "More milk" — which in turn becomes the complete sentence — "I want more milk" — probably by around age three in normal children. A rapid increase in vocabulary occurs during the eighteen-month to two-year period with many of the added words being nouns — names of things — as the child acquires more and more answers to his favorite question, "What's that?" Verbs enter his vocabulary a little more slowly; modifiers still more slowly. Phrases and conjunctions appear between three and a half and four and a half years of age.

Meanings too are gradually extended. The two-year-old, seeing a tiger at the zoo, may say "kitty," using the name he knows to apply to the animal which seems similar. The four-year-old, wise from exposure to stories and pictures, may say "That's a tiger." He is able to use the more specific term because he has had more experience, more living time, and more information. The still older child, perhaps ten or eleven, wanting to keep the peace, may say, "Well, you're both right, in a way — tiger or kitty, they're both animals." He has reached a still higher level of generalization and categorization.

Speech and language development is crucial in the educational process. Language is considered the most important single factor in problem solving. It makes possible combining and relating ideas. With it, one can move from the here-and-now, concrete, object level of communication to the symbolic and abstract levels. Language is important also in social experience and social interaction and hence significantly affects personality development. Rightly, the appearance and progress of speech are matters of deep concern to parents.

Mental retardation is the most common cause of delayed speech (the child who doesn't learn to talk at the expected age, at least by the age of two) and of defective speech (defective both in articulation and in structure). In some mentally retarded children there may have been specific damage to the part of the brain most related to speech development. Sensory handicaps — in vision, hearing, and motor ability — also affect the development of speech and language. The totally deaf child acquires speech, if at all, only through highly specialized teaching and tremendous effort; even then, his speech is likely to be hard to understand, lacking in expression, and very limited in abstract content. The hard-of-hearing child, even though not totally deaf, will have trouble with articulation, sound discrimination, accuracy of imitation, and sorting out meanings of words which are different but between which he cannot adequately discriminate. The blind child is also likely to have problems in speech and language because of his inability to see and observe others speaking, as well as because of the limitations his lack of vision puts on his social experiences. The child with a motor defect may, or may not, have problems in language, but he may very well have difficulty in the actual motor production of speech. The child with a cleft palate will have problems in speech production and in voice quality. In addition the child who falls into the autistic or childhood schizophrenic zones of emotional and personality deviation, functioning at a retarded level whatever his presumed native capacity may be, may acquire speech but not be able to use it normally for communication purposes. As noted earlier, one or more of these handicaps often accompany mental retardation, thus further limiting the development of speech.

The speech of the mentally retarded child will match his mental-age level more closely than it matches his chronological-age level. By the age of seven, normal children have outgrown most of their speech immaturities. It takes about this long for most children to have mastered some of the more difficult sound combinations. Retarded children who are developing mentally at from one-third to one-half of the normal rate (the trainable group) will still be very immature in speech when they enter school. If they start school at six, their speech skills will be similar to those of the two- to three-year-old child. When they are twelve, and their mental maturity levels are for the most part between four and six years of age, their speech immaturities will still be with them. The situation of the educable group, developing at from one-half to three-fourths of the normal rate, is a little more hopeful. They will also be immature in speech at age six, when mentally they are between three and four and a half. Some of them will still have articulation problems when they are twelve chronologically and mentally between six and nine years of age. Mental growth is a little more on their side, however; in general, they will outgrow their speech immaturities a little faster.

For all the retarded, we need to consider the role of habit. Once a child has learned to talk at all, his own talking reinforces the inaccuracies of his articulation and pronunciation. Even though his vocabulary and his comprehension increase, in keeping with the increase in his mental capacity, his articulation may stay about the same because he practices his mistakes too thoroughly. Also, if two-word sentences have been adequate for his communication needs, he is likely to continue to use them and not try to develop more complex language skills.

Some parents place much importance on their retarded child learning to read. But they should ask themselves whether this will be useful knowledge for the retardate. Children first learn to recognize single words. This is like picture recognition; a step in reading, but not really reading. A child has a simple pre-primer, with repetitive content and pictures. It says, "Look, Dick, look. See Jane run. See Jane jump." Along with this are pictures of Dick and Jane and their activities. It doesn't take too long for the child to remember the story connected with the pictures. This is association of pictures with words, plus rote memory. Useful reading begins with memorized words; it progresses to a point where the child can use what he knows to get at what he doesn't know. Familiarity with letter sounds helps unlock new words. If he knows that "c-a-t" means "cat," he can figure out that "m-a-t" means "mat," because he knows that "m-a-n" means "man." The inflexibility and inability to generalize, traits so typical of the retarded, become important here. A retarded child doesn't know how to guess intelligently. The normal child may confront a word he doesn't know, but because he has some comprehension of the content, he can make a good guess. A trainable child may be taught to recognize forty or fifty new words over the course of several years, but we should consider whether the time devoted to this effort might better have been spent giving him some knowledge he could put to better use.

Many parents hope that speech therapy will help their retarded child. There are, however, some special problems in working with the retarded on speech correction. Brief periods of practice, which are helpful for children of normal ability, do not offset for the retarded child the long periods of incorrect practice. To be effective, speech therapy requires that the child be able to discriminate between sounds in order to hear the differences. Making auditory discriminations requires more mental maturity than many retarded children have. Retarded children are not as intrinsically motivated to improve their speech as normal children usually are. They are not as self-critical; they are less able to make discriminations; often they have been overprotected by parents, and not encouraged to grow up and become more self-sufficient in a multitude of ways. Many times, they are more self-centered and really not interested in whether or not they can communicate. Almost always, they have less self-motivation to make an effort in specific discrimination learning so the therapist has to try to supply motivation from the outside.

Some children, even though retarded, can and do benefit from individual and small-group speech therapy. Among these are children with hearing defects or cleft palates and those with brain-damage patterns which have directly affected speech development. A useful criterion of how speech therapy should be used is the comparison of a child's speech — articulation, structure, and content — with his general level of mental maturity. For the majority of retarded children, whose level of speech is in keeping with their ability level, speech therapy will have limited value. It should be considered, however, for children whose communication skills are markedly below their general level of mental maturity.

There is a more useful approach for most retarded children than a twenty-minute period of individual speech therapy twice weekly: incorporation of speech and language teaching into every activity that goes on in the classroom. The speech therapist can contribute more to the speech develop-

ment of retarded children by spending time helping classroom teachers understand where to start, and what to do,
in encouraging children to improve their production of specific sounds than by taking on three or four children for individual treatment. The role of the speech therapist here is
to provide for teachers information on the normal sequences
of learning and sound production and guidance on the "right"
developmental approach to take, rather than trying to turn
teachers into speech therapists.

An essential point for parents bears repeating: in general,
speech and language skills are very closely connected to general mental development. When there is a marked discrepancy between the mental level of a child and the level of
his communication skills, the expert help of a speech correctionist is needed. When no real discrepancy exists, a speech
correctionist really cannot do much. Rather, continuing attention should be paid to the social aspects of speech, communication between child and child, child and adult, along with
classroom practice and encouraging comprehensible speech
throughout every classroom activity.

There are also some helpful practices parents can follow.
An important one is not to imitate the child's inaccuracies
or imperfections. Just because he says he wants some "gwavy"
is not an excuse for the parent, who may be amused by this
immaturity, to ask him if he wants some more "gwavy." You
can at least set him a good example; say the words correctly
so he has a model to imitate. Parents should also attempt to
encourage talking. Again, example is part of this; help provide as much language stimulation as possible by talking to
the child, listening to him, giving him a busy and meaningful
language environment. It is better to encourage the child to
talk more, especially when he is quite young, than it is to
be too critical of how he talks. The goal is to develop skill in
communication rather than perfect articulation. Too much

criticism can make the child quit trying altogether. Don't talk baby talk to the child. Surely a six-year-old, even if he is only three mentally, is kept in an infant stage longer by the mother who asks him at dinner time if he wants some "yum-yum" instead of telling him that dinner is ready, or asking if he wants some more carrots. If we want to help our retarded children to be socially acceptable, we need to keep in mind terminology appropriate for their ages. We shouldn't ask six-year-olds if they want to "go potty." In other words, in the development of speech, parents of a retarded child who "over-accept" the retardation and expect nothing from the child can do as much harm as parents who refuse to accept the retardation and constantly try to force the child to do things which are beyond him.

8 *THE IMPORTANCE OF FEELINGS*

RETARDED children's feelings are seldom realistically discussed in books and articles. Reliable information is available about the emotional development of children generally, and one can find useful suggestions for treating some specific emotional problems — how to "cure" a child of being afraid of dogs or thunderstorms, or how to extinguish temper tantrums. But when people do talk about the feelings of retarded children, the factual basis for what they say is difficult to identify. For example, it has been said that retarded children have the same feelings as other children. I consider this an incomplete, if not an untrue, statement. What feelings mean to a person is related to what he can interpret and think about his feelings. Retarded children do have feelings and emotional capacity, but it seems likely to me that they do not develop their emotional capacity to the same degree or with the same differentiation as do normal children.

From developmental studies, we know that babies have a general emotional capacity. They do not feel anything as specific as love, hate, jealousy, anger; they simply have a response to stimulation, an "excitement" response. As they live longer and learn from experience, the more specific responses develop from their generalized capacity. Normal children, even at quite early ages, do some thinking about how they feel and why they feel that way. A normal child can tell you, by the time he is four or five, when he is angry and what he is angry about. The retarded child can indicate by his behavior that something is disturbing him, but the interpretation of anger or fear or whatever is made by the observer, not the child. This is an important difference. One element here is the problem of language — the retarded child may not have the words to express his feelings: but we must also keep in mind that he lacks comprehension, to some degree, too.

It is possible that damage to the brain, responsible for much mental retardation, can affect parts of the brain involved with emotional functioning as readily as parts involved with intellectual functioning. Some children known to have had brain damage show emotional patterns that are deviant, distorted, and hard to modify. It seems reasonable to speculate that some of these traits may result from a damaged emotional organization. Some people have assumed that emotions are the same across the wide range of individual intellectual differences, but this may not be true at all. We simply do not know whether retarded children have the same emotional capacity as normal children.

We must, nevertheless, recognize the importance of feelings for the retarded youngster, as for us all. Even if we can't be sure of the exact nature or extent of his emotions, we know that they do exist and they do influence his behavior. We also know that, just as many of the emotional responses of normal youngsters are learned responses, so too at least some of the emotional patterns of mentally retarded children are conditioned by their early experiences.

Among mentally retarded children, there are many fearful, timid youngsters who seem young for their age, even when compared with other retarded children. They are dependent, babyish, and frightened. They seem afraid to reach out to anything in their environment, almost literally afraid to touch anything. Often they cling to a person, a place, or a thing. They frequently stand in a corner because they feel safer there. They don't have many interests. They are, however, treatable in a school situation, and usually respond rather quickly. What helps them is experience; they must be given gradual exposure to things they can feel safe with, which will build up their confidence until finally they can try something new and move out of their corner. Then one sees them ex-panding — generally not into very self-confident youngsters, but into youngsters with a much greater ability than before to enjoy and to participate in what is around them. Timid children usually aren't difficult to live with if their parents don't mind having them be so dependent. Most parents who have this type of child don't mind the dependency — which is part of the reason they are dependent. Even though the fear-ful child isn't hard to live with, one wonders what his life is like, and whether or not he is happy.

At an extreme, the dependent child is more than timid; he is frozen. For him, treatment in the school situation is more difficult and takes more time. Often this child has had a lim-ited background of social experience. New experiences are important in helping him, but he also needs an "accepting" teacher, one willing to let him be the way he is for quite a while. The other children ask why Danny stands by the door, and the accepting teacher tells them, "He feels better there — he'll come to the table when he's ready." Danny hears this. It may be that he doesn't believe it yet, but little by little he moves toward the group.

Another child may show a mixture of fear and bossiness. Although on the surface he acts like a dictator, underneath he is frightened. Often this child is one whose retardation stems from organic damage. He is rigid, can't tolerate change, can't adapt. He can feel safe only when he is the "boss," but inwardly he is too frightened to be the "boss" and doesn't really know what to do with his authority. This child is difficult to manage. Other children are afraid of him; he looks quite convincing in his role of dictator to others in his age group. He isn't as convincing to his teacher, but it's hard to know where to cut into this cycle. If you threaten his control, you increase his fear and he goes to pieces. If you try to do something about his fear, you threaten his control, and he goes to pieces in another way. He is a puzzling child and a solution to his problems requires time, consistent and fair handling, and perhaps some good luck.

The stubborn child, at first glance, seems simpler to deal with. He will say "no" to anything he is asked; he has committed himself to the denial of all authority. This may stem from the normal negativistic stage of childhood. The normal two-year-old, with limited language and a developmental need to define himself as a person and secure some autonomy, often behaves this way but usually outgrows it in six months or a year. At six years of age the retarded child, who mentally may be still verging on age three, has had extended practice with the effectiveness of negativism. If one believes at all in the role of habit, or in the likelihood that behavior which has brought rewards in the past will be repeated, it makes good sense that a negativistic child will not suddenly become cooperative when for several years he has been rewarded for not being cooperative. There are some solutions to this problem. One is to limit, deliberately, the demands that are made of him. This may seem like letting him go his own way, but it really isn't. Think through the requests that you make of him, choose a few that seem most crucial to you, and limit the demands to these few. What they should be depends on the family situation. Once you have chosen the few crucial things, hold the line on these and don't offer or permit a choice. Not offering a child a choice if he really doesn't have one is a simple principle, but a hard one to follow. Parents come to our playroom at Sheltering Arms where their child is having a wonderful time exploring new toys and games, and ask him, "Do you want to go home now?" Of course he says, "No." A child should not be given a choice unless he is allowed to make the choice. If he isn't allowed to choose, why make it appear that he is, and then contradict his choice? Give him choices when he really has a choice; don't give him a choice if you intend to make it for him.

The hostile, aggressive child presents difficulties both at school and at home. In some ways he is like the fearful but bossy child; he may be very frightened underneath the bluff of his exterior attitude. His attacks are often completely unprovoked; this way he can win more frequently because he catches people off guard. Sometimes this child is revengeful: he is striking back at something in his experience that has seemed unfair. The unfairness may not be objectively true, but if it seems true to him, it can affect his behavior. This child is often self-centered, has learned no real social awareness, and has had too little good experience. He is frequently socially immature, having had too much adult attention and solicitude or not enough give-and-take with other children. It isn't always undesirable for a child to become aggressive at school. Children need to test out their feelings, and it is healthy for them to do it in a group the right size with a teacher who understands what this is all about. You have to be able to stand back and watch children to appreciate what's going on inside them. But if a child is very hostile and aggressive, he's an unhappy child and needs help.

When we attempt to discover why retarded children feel and act in these ways, we find that one of the contributing factors is parental attitude. The parents of retarded children are haunted by such questions as these: What should I expect? What should I do? Where should I go for help? Some want to make it up to the child for being retarded and overprotect him. Others try to overcome the retardation by constant pressure on the child to improve. Many are confused and vacillate in their approach to the child. All this influences a child's emotional reactions. We can make some generalizations. Overprotective parents are more likely to have children who are fearful, timid, and dependent. Parents who determinedly use heavy pressure to "make" the child behave and conform are more likely to have resistive, rebellious, angry children. Parents who can't make up their minds what approach to follow are more likely to have children who are confused in their feelings and behavior. Of course the attitudes of others than parents — teachers, playmates, society at large — also have an influence. And I want to reiterate my belief that there may be significant organic damage to the emotional equipment in some mentally retarded children.

However it comes about, many mentally retarded children do have serious emotional problems of one sort or another. These must be viewed in the context of what we usually call "personality development," for personality is organized around emotions. In the field of mental retardation, we may not have paid enough attention to the idea that normal personality development involves normal ability, that the degree to which a retarded child can attain what would be defined as normal personality is limited by his intellectual lack. Perhaps this area has been neglected because we aren't entirely certain how personality does develop or what theoretical framework is most adequate to describe it.

One formulation of personality development useful in thinking about children describes several developmental tasks. As his first personality task, the infant must develop a sense of trust in other people. He develops this during the first year of his life, as people take care of him, feed him, keep him comfortable, play with him, talk to him, and respond to him.

When he cries, they are there. This engenders a sense of trust. The second stage, the development of a sense of autonomy, goes on between the ages of about one and three years. It is during these years that the child discovers himself as a separate person. He grabs the spoon when his mother is feeding him and announces, "Me do." He gradually establishes the fact that he will be independent and can master his environment. He can't accomplish this entirely, of course, since he is small, immature, inept, and inexperienced. But it is important for his development that there be things in his environment that he *can* master; this is why parents encourage young children to walk, to explore, to play, to try things out. The sense of initiative develops from about age three to five. The child now is imitative; he wants to participate, to do what others are doing, to learn. He is eager and has many ideas about what he wants to do. Some of them he can't do, and he will need support and reassurance from his parents. If the child at the stage of autonomy exclaims, "I am me," at the stage of initiative he asserts, "I want to." The beginning of the school years ushers in the stage of "I can do" and "I have done." This stage is marked by a sense of accomplishment and is generally a smoother time for children. Earlier, there are so many things he really can't do, and his experiments and efforts often lead to some negative parental reaction.

Obviously, mental retardation is going to affect how fully and effectively each of these "senses" can be developed. The retarded infant probably fares reasonably well at the first stage — for one thing his retardation would usually not yet be evident and he is probably treated much like a normal child; the retardation would not in itself usually prevent him from developing a sense of trust. But beginning with the second stage, the retarded youngster encounters more difficulty than the normal child and is likely to experience more and more failures. By school age many retarded children show fear of failure and reluctance to try anything new. Given the innate lack of intellectual capacity in retardates, a great number of failures cannot be avoided, and personality development in the mentally retarded, it seems to me, cannot be "normal." But we can do more than we have done to prevent some of the secondary emotional problems from developing, to make learned emotional responses positive rather than negative. Success is, partly, a matter of definition. If a parent defines something as a failure, the child will consider it a failure; if, on the other hand, the parent finds an aspect to praise as success, the child will have something positive to build on. Successes are essential for every child; since his first years are spent at home, every effort should be made by parents to find things at which he can be successful.

A child's self-awareness and insight are related to ability level, but the correlation is far from perfect. Some trainable ability children are acutely aware of their shortcomings; some educable children are remarkably blind to theirs. It is not true that the closer the child is to normal ability, the more aware he is of his limitations. Sensitivity has something to do with this, and no one is quite sure how to define or measure sensitivity. We often hear older educable youngsters expressing anxiety about their future. There is an upswing in this anxiety as children approach a school transition, especially if it is to a junior high school special program. They are worried about competition and about being able to do the work. If they have a speech problem, they worry whether their new teacher will be able to understand them. They worry about making friends. The teacher can be helpful at this point, not by offering false reassurance, but by realistic discussion. She may say something like "That's why we are working on your independent study skills right now, so that next year you'll be able to do these things by yourself." She manages to show them that current experience is related to future experience.

Older children may express some feelings, usually negative ones, about being retarded. They say, "I just hate being retarded," or "Why do I have to be retarded?" Parents and teachers often haven't been sure how to help a retarded child accept his retardation. They may try to avoid the word and make excuses for the child. I believe that such a denial by adults whom the child trusts is dangerous and may take away the last prop he has for his self-respect. Some people, even teachers, say to a child, "You can do it if you try." Often this is completely untrue. He *can't* do it if he tries; trying harder isn't the answer. He only has so much with which to try, and to give him the idea that when he fails it is because he didn't try hard enough seems not only unrealistic but cruel. We are more likely to contribute to the child's emotional health if we realistically accept the fact that not everyone can do everything, interpret this to the child, and help him identify the things he can do.

Some children express a fear of growing up, or a wish not to grow up. "I don't want to grow up," "I don't want to go to a different school," or "I don't want to have a job." Such a comment suggests that the speaker is aware of shortcomings and doesn't know where he fits or where he is going to fit. We don't always know just where he will fit, so reassurance has to be somewhat general — "There are lots of different things you might like to do." We can describe some aspects of various programs which might be suitable and available. Reassurance is false unless it is based on honesty. Retarded children very often have some very honest feelings; we can do them no greater harm than to deny the honesty of their feelings.

Feelings or emotions can be described as the fuel which makes the motor run. The motor — the person's capacity, ability level, what he has to work with — won't start unless it gets fuel; when the fuel reaches it, the motor runs toward

accomplishment, learning, achievement. School should make
the fuel flow more freely, even — or perhaps especially — for
the retarded child. If the teacher, whether in a special class
or a special school, is skillful and sensitive, the school will be
a secure place, where the child feels that people accept him
and he belongs. There are things to do, and he likes to do
them. Success can be variously defined: effort can mean success; progress can mean success. School provides companions
and comparisons. The retarded child can do some things better than some of his classmates, and other things not as well.
Someone may hit him, and he may cry, but the next minute
they are hugging each other. In the older groups, battles become more verbal; children get their feelings hurt. But this
is life. They are having social experiences and are learning
to get along with other people. They are neither isolated nor
ignored nor overprotected.

There can't be too many rules in a class or school for retarded children. If there are too many rules, there are too
many broken rules. Too many broken rules are likely to mean
too much punishment; too much punishment undercuts motivation. Without motivation, a child won't make the effort
of which he is capable; without effort, there can't be success.
Without success, there is little progress. Fundamental rules
stress safety, supervision, justice. The concern must be with
control rather than punishment. Teachers must try to keep
children's behavior within the limits considered reasonable,
and to keep children from doing too many "wrong" things
so punishment can be avoided. Essentially, this is a philosophy
of "preventive discipline" which does not deny the child the
right to be a person and to have some freedom. There must
be concern about helping children accept themselves better.
If a teacher likes a child, he can like himself better. If his classmates like him, he can like himself better too. Part of his liking
himself better comes about because his feelings are not de-

nied; what he feels is what he feels. We may try to redirect his feelings or interpret them, or explain them, or, over time, to change them — but we do not deny them. He has a right to his feelings, in school and in other places. Channeling his feelings in positive directions is the task of the school as well as of his parents.

9 CAPITALIZING ON THE SOCIAL ASSETS

IT IS in the development of retarded children's social skills that parents can make really noticeable changes and produce some good results. Concerning parent-child relationships, someone has said that since the beginning of time, there has been a battle between the generations: the parents determined to "civilize" their offspring, the children resistant to being civilized. Infants are notably unconcerned about other people. They are self-centered little creatures who demand, and get, care. The saving thing is that they *do* have the capacity to learn to care about other people. A little later, parents get some help with the civilizing, socializing jobs. Schools come into the picture; Sunday school, Boy Scouts, Girl Scouts, and Campfire Girls, as well as other sources of authority, all have roles to play as children grow a little older and venture beyond their homes for some of their growing-up experiences. It is still the parents, however, who lay the basic foundations.

Whether normal, gifted, or retarded, all children have to go through the socializing process, but mentally retarded children differ in at least two ways. One way is that retardation carries with it limitation on the ability to learn; the limitation is most conspicuous in intellectual, academic learning, but to some extent, it is there in every kind of learning.

Learning what is acceptable, learning conformity, learning to adapt, learning to make use of experience — these are all harder for retardates than for normal children. The degree of retardation forecasts, with some accuracy, how much more difficult any kind of learning will be for the child. While the correlation between intelligence level and social adjustment is not perfect, it is considerable.

Second, retarded children are likely to have other handicaps. A good example is the extreme hyperactivity and over-response to stimulation of a brain-injured child during his early years. Socially, this child has an extra burden. Other people think, and sometimes say, "Good heavens, can't those parents control that child?" The parents may react by shutting the door against the outside world and choosing to live in social isolation to protect themselves and their child against criticism. Or they may react by exerting even more pressure on their child to try to force him to be "normal." Even if the retarded child has no secondary handicaps, his parents tend to overprotect him or make constant demands on him — or vacillate from one attitude to the other, as we have seen. Either way, the child's personality is affected, and this in turn will influence his social development. By the time he gets to school he may have serious social liabilities.

What is a social liability? An important one that is especially common among young retarded children is self-centeredness, lack of awareness of other people. The selfish child who expresses himself in controlling behavior and tantrums is resented by the other children because he spoils everyone's fun. The extremely resistive, negativistic child is not welcome in a social group. There are youngsters who are so negative that they almost say "No" before you ask them anything. The child who is destructive makes himself unpopular. It isn't just his own things that he destroys — he destroys other people's things, too. The child who whines, cries, and has no "give and take" skills is also hard to have around. We expect some disobedience; most retarded children fail to conform to requests some of the time. However, the child who almost never obeys is deeply resented by others. These traits are important not only in comparing retarded children with normal children, but also when all the children in the group are retarded. In this latter situation, the child who is rejected by his peers is the one who spoils the activity, runs off with the ball, won't play by the rules, won't wait for his turn, or somehow breaks up the project which others are enjoying. Some children do not evoke real rejection by their peers as much as indifference. Often these are the children who show some of the "autistic" traits. They don't care about the things others enjoy. They may not be actively rejected, but little by little, others pay less attention to them because they get so little response. Some rejected children are rejected because they talk too much; some because they can't keep up or perform well enough in some activity or pursuit, or because they interfere, or are indifferent.

One of the problems of older retarded people often is that their social behavior in groups is inappropriate — it is too different from what others are doing. They make faces; they do silly things, or giggle, or talk too much, or demand too much attention, or somehow make people uncomfortable. Acceptance is very much related to whether others are made uncomfortable by what the retarded person is doing. Many retardates have poor communication skills. We often can't do much to improve a speech defect. This may make other people very uncomfortable. If a retardate is trying to say something to someone else who can't understand what he is saying, this creates an awkwardness. The listener doesn't know what to do about it; he doesn't know how to improve the situation, so he goes away or turns aside — he rejects the defective speaker because he himself is embarrassed. You may have had a similar experience in talking with visitors from other countries. Difficulty in communication increases tension. The harder you try to communicate with the other person, the more tense, anxious, and uncomfortable you become.

Probably no retarded person can be socially effective or socially sought after as normal persons would use these terms, but many of them can be socially acceptable, and this is the goal. We don't expect them to be outstanding, to be the star of the show, but we can anticipate that many of them will be able to blend with their setting, their associates, their co-workers, and not stand out as being too different in appearance or behavior. With this in mind, how can parents cultivate the social assets and diminish the liabilities?

First of all, parents should promote independence and self-help skills both in behavior and in attitude. Avoid being, or feeling, overprotective. Take the extra time needed for the child to do things for himself. When he must be helped, help him, but don't do the whole thing for him. Help only as much as needed to enable the child to finish the job himself. This takes self-analysis and observation because you have lived with your habits for years, and you aren't aware of what you habitually do unless you make a real effort to watch and listen to yourself.

Give him responsibilities at home — small ones, maybe, but real ones. Of course you'll have to remind him, and you'll say that it really is easier to do what needs to be done yourself. Don't. Work instead toward the day that he doesn't need reminding.

Don't always take his part in conflicts with other children, either your normal children or his playmates outside the family. Let them work out some problems for themselves. You don't go running if two of your normal children are having a scrap. If your retarded child is outdoors and you hear the sound of battle, your feeling probably is, "Oh, I'd better see what's wrong." You should probably take a look, to assess the situation, but if it is a fair sort of squabble, try to stay out of it.

Help your retarded child accept himself as a person, and help him be a person. Don't deny that he is different, when he brings the question up as he probably will. When retarded children ask, "Am I retarded?" there is only one answer you can honestly give. If you are not honest, you will lose the child's confidence anyhow. Although you shouldn't deny the handicap, you can still help the child feel that he is worthy, valued, respected. The more things he can do for himself and the greater the independence he has acquired, the easier it is to build on these feelings of self-worth when he becomes a job applicant as an adult. Avoid giving him too much personal, individual attention because this makes him think that everyone will provide it wherever he goes. When he enters school and finds that the teacher is not just for him, he may have trouble accepting the situation. If he has been "revolved around" with smothering, careful, watchful, loving, concerned, anxious, worried, fearful parents, he has no way of knowing that the rest of the world may be different.

A happy, cooperative disposition is an asset to a retarded child. The child who smiles and laughs readily and has some sense of humor will fit more readily with a group than the angry child who strikes out at others without provocation. If your retarded child is aggressive, it may be helpful to take note of the findings of a study of normal preschool children and their mothers' attitudes. The study found that mothers who felt that they were very permissive, who said, in effect, "If he wants to hit me, he can hit me, because I understand how he feels," had children who were very aggressive. Mothers who were very punishing, who said, "I would never permit my child to hit me; under no circumstances would I tolerate this," also had children who were very aggressive. The children who were least aggressive had mothers who were neither permissive nor punitive. These mothers said something like this: "I don't really believe my child has any right to hit me, and I don't intend to let him," but they found other ways to get around the behavior. If one of these children came up and hit his mother, she probably took his hand and said, "Let's go for a walk," or used some other diverting tactics, coupled with a reminder, "You are not allowed to hit me." But she didn't use retaliative punishment.

Punishment is satisfying to parents for they feel that then they are doing something to control the child and make him act better. Yet it very often reinforces the behavior that they wish to prevent because by the time the child has been aggressive, he has already gotten fun out of it and the fun was his reward. The punishment comes too late and does not always deter him from trying again. If punishment is severe enough or frequent enough, it may drive the behavior "underground" or into some other area, but by itself, punishment is not likely to solve the problem. Among other things, the child who is punished excessively is likely to become anxious, and then we have two sets of emotional disturbance—the hostile set that makes him want to be aggressive, and the anxious, worried set that makes him feel guilty about it. It seems reasonable to assume that neither permissiveness nor punitiveness is desirable in encouraging socially acceptable behavior in retarded children.

Being good at something, being able to excel, is a social asset. A little boy who can print people's names on the blackboard better than others in his group gets a lift from this. The child who can roller skate, jump rope, or excel in any skill, relative to his group, can turn this to social advantage. It may not matter too much what it is, but every child benefits from a feeling that he is "good at this"—whatever "this" may be. If he can't find something to be good at, he may seek satisfaction by going in the other direction and finding something "bad" to do. At least this gets him attention.

Ability to take turns, to share, is another asset. Some rigid children have trouble with this. They can't change their pace or shift their activity. It may not matter that the retarded child understands *why* he should share; the important thing is that he learns to do it. He needs to be able to take turns and share with some graciousness a majority of the time by age nine or so, or we have failed him in a very important way.

In older children, it is an asset to be somewhat inconspicuous. This means conformity in dress, manner, and in general reaction to what the group is doing. An older, bigger child looks inappropriate on a tricycle, even though he is having trouble learning to ride a bicycle. You might ask, "What difference does it make, if he enjoys it and just rides it at school?" It makes a difference in how he feels about himself. If he thinks of himself as a tricycle rider at age twelve or thirteen, we have failed somehow to help him develop a better image of himself as a person. We have to move him ahead in social maturity or other people will look at him with disdain.

We can identify three stages in social acceptance for retarded children. First, we would like them not to be rejected by other people with real hostility feelings. This is the minimal goal. Beyond this, we would like them to be tolerated by others, accepted at some level, perhaps with an attitude of "He's all right; I don't mind having him around." Even more, we would like our retarded children to be genuinely liked and enjoyed by other people. We have to keep in mind that acceptability of behavior is not an absolute concept. What is acceptable in one family may not be acceptable in another; what is normal behavior in one neighborhood is not considered normal in another. Consequently, whether or not a retarded child is accepted in his immediate environment is dependent on his environment as well as on the child.

Parents can't change the retarded child's potential; they can't give him more ability; they can't always control all of his behavior. In social learning, however, where experience, training, and attitude are so important, parents can make a very positive contribution in helping their children learn how to get along comfortably with other people within their environment — and it is well worth it.

10 MAKING BETTER USE OF PROFESSIONAL HELP

ALL parents of mentally retarded children have been exposed to various professional services. How you who are parents feel about the ones you have received probably ranges from very dissatisfied to very well pleased. It may be useful to look at the total picture of professional services for retarded children to see what parents themselves might do to make them more helpful.

First, we need to recognize that parent defensiveness often gets in the way of making the best use of available professional help. Some parents are not willing or able to admit the problems they have with their child. Quite often, the parent of an applicant for admission to a special school will say that there are simply no problems at home. Then, as parent and child are leaving, the parent will add: "I just don't know what I will do if he has to be home next year." It is difficult enough to admit to yourself that you don't know how to cope with your own child; it is even more difficult to admit it to someone else. But if you can't say it, in some way, how can you expect help?

Some parents can't admit there is a problem because they can't see it. They have adapted so completely to living the child's life for him that a problem just doesn't become visible.

After all, if a child is dressed every morning as a matter of course, the parent doesn't know that he can't dress himself. His mother might say, "I'm sure he could do this. It's my fault; I never taught him. It's just easier to do it for him." Parents tend to identify themselves with their child; the parent has lived a lot of the child's life out of necessity or convenience. If a mother admits to a problem, it reflects on her. Somehow she is less than a good parent if she has any trouble with this child. Consequently, problems aren't recognizable.

Over time, there is also discouragement. In the early years of the child's life, parents have often made great efforts to understand him, to get help for him, to help him be "normal," and finally they reach the point where it is easier to live with the problems than to try to change. He's got to have chocolate milk or he isn't happy; he's got to have the hall light on at night or he isn't happy. Parents tolerate many demands because this is easier than trying to change the child through changing their own behavior. None of us likes to modify our own behavior very much; it is easier to keep on doing as we have been doing. But with a retarded child there is this difference: here we are dealing with another person whose life is being affected by our behavior.

Some parents are unable even to accept the fact that their child could be retarded. This fences them in very firmly. If you deny the reality of the situation, you won't be able to communicate with anyone because you won't be talking about the same circumstances. But the reality of the child, what he is and what he can do, will still exist. Some parents are in conflict between themselves about the retardation. Often it is the father who is the denying parent, but sometimes it is the mother. There are degrees of denying the problem. One extreme is to deny the retardation entirely; the child is all right, the world is wrong. Another degree is to admit that the child has problems now, but to believe that they are only temporary.

He'll "catch up" at age twelve, or "wake up" one of these days. Intellectually, you know better, but you don't know what to do then so you cling to the magic myth that the child will suddenly be made over. Try to cultivate some objectivity, to look at your child as an individual, apart from you. As parents, try to communicate with each other. Many parents of retarded children have never been able to talk with each other openly about the retardation and their feelings about it. This can mean that parents drift farther and farther apart in their thinking. It also means, usually, that professional help essential to a retarded child's welfare either is not sought or is not used effectively.

As has already been noted, retardation crosses many professional lines; it is not the province of any one field. The medical area covers not only the routine physical examination, but also the specialty services — neurology, psychiatry, physiology, biochemistry, audiology, visual studies, dental care, and genetic studies. Not every child receives every service, but under full medical coverage, ideally, he should. Psychological services include ability measurements and, depending on the age of the child, personality measurements and observations, vocational or prevocational tests. There may be a speech and language evaluation. Social work is concerned with the family situation, the child's past experience, and the interrelationships of home and school. Educational settings provide the basic school learning experiences, and, as the child grows older, vocational evaluations, job training, placement, and supervision. Some retarded children need additional help in physical and occupational therapy. Most can benefit by special recreational provisions, camping programs, and religious education.

Let us look at the medical area first. With normal children, use of all available diagnostic services may not be as essential as for retarded children. Parents of normal children rely largely on regular checkups and immunizations, and take good health for granted much of the time; when special diagnostic tests are needed, such children can usually cooperate and understand. The retarded child is less able to understand what's going on and is further handicapped by not being able to express what he feels. He can't describe his symptoms, or explain his response; often he doesn't know what is expected of him. If the doctor testing his hearing says, "Tell me when you hear a sound," the child may not comprehend this request. This introduces a margin of error in some diagnostic procedures. The retarded child is limited in comprehension and in making discriminations. It isn't until he reaches a mental age of about four years that he can understand the concepts of "same" and "different," and even then his understanding is concrete and limited. In any diagnostic procedure which requires the child's cooperation, results will be suspect to the degree that the child is unable to comprehend. Some tests are not so dependent on the child's participation, and results of these are less suspect.

With retarded children, as with normal children, if any problem is superimposed on another problem there are more than two problems. A child who is mentally retarded and also visually handicapped does not have just two problems; he has two problems which interrelate with and affect each other, so the total effect is more than two single handicaps. With retarded children, it is especially important to study and identify other defects which may exist in addition to the retardation.

Every child who is retarded should have a thorough medical evaluation as soon as a developmental problem is apparent. This entails the complete battery of all the blood tests, endocrine tests, neurological tests — everything that can contribute to understanding the cause of the retardation. Some tests are of more limited meaning with very young children; an EEG given to a one-year-old generally doesn't mean quite the same thing as an EEG given to a five-year-old. Other tests, however, are of special importance in the first months of a child's life. A thyroid deficiency, for example, needs to be identified as early as possible so that thyroid extract can be given to prevent further damage. If a child happens to be one of those with phenylketenuria, early diagnosis is crucial because dietary treatment can help prevent further damage. Both of these conditions are quite rare, but there is no way of knowing at the time for which children it would be safe to omit the identifying tests. Obviously, when major medical problems become evident, medical diagnosis should be sought immediately. Most parents whose children have convulsive disorders or severe problems of health, development, eating, or sleeping have quickly taken them to the doctor's office. The children who have not had thorough medical study are likely to be those whose problems, whatever they were, didn't look to the parents like medical problems.

Even the most expert and complete medical diagnosis will rarely be able to undo retardation. Even so, most parents are more comfortable with their situation when they know as much as can be known about the cause of retardation in their child. Many conditions can be improved through treatment. Some endocrine problems are treatable; some blood sugar problems can be improved; a child with a convulsive disorder can be greatly helped by medication which controls the convulsions. If a child has a vision problem and it is corrected with glasses, he will be able to use his ability, at whatever level it exists, more effectively. If he has a hearing defect, early detection and treatment will have a significant impact on development of the child's language skills. Some children who have never had a seizure or outward evidence of a convulsive disorder, but who do have an abnormal EEG pattern suggestive of convulsive activity in the brain, benefit by anticonvulsant medication. It probably won't improve their intelligence test scores, but they often function better, behave better, and use their ability more purposefully.

How parents obtain thorough medical study depends partly on where they live. In most metropolitan areas, full medical studies are available either through general hospitals, specialized clinics, or arrangements made by a pediatrician. In smaller towns and rural areas, it may be a more difficult process, but it is still possible if parents feel it to be important. Even in urban areas, parents will encounter problems in obtaining medical as well as other professional help. There are likely to be transportation problems, communication problems, telephone problems. You've probably all had the experience of being ready to move toward some kind of help. You pick up the phone, dial a number, and the line is busy. Immediately you feel a sense of relief — "I tried, and couldn't get them." Or you call to make an appointment to have your child studied, and find that the calendar is full until January. This "takes you off the hook" and you let things slide until another problem alarms you. If you want some professional help in an urban area, you will probably have to cultivate persistence and determination. Although there are many sources of help, it is difficult to know which one you need; it is true that often you will have to wait. But if you really want help, you'll persist. If you think you want it, but aren't persisting, look again at your motivations.

A minimal essential medical program should include an annual physical examination following the full-scale medical study. Immunizations and booster shots should be kept up to date. For a child on any medication, there should be regular follow-ups — how frequently depends on the condition for which the medication is being given. There should be regular vision and hearing tests. For children in school, these are often given on a "screening" basis to select children needing further study. Many young retarded children, especially in the trainable groups, are not able to cooperate with the screening procedures, and the result is a report that says, "Test unreliable." For these children, further study is indicated. Dental checkups are important. Not all dentists choose to work with retarded children, but some do. Often your local Association for Retarded Children can steer you toward appropriate help.

Parents are responsible for giving their child the advantages of medical diagnostic study and routine medical attention. You also are responsible for participating in this process. To make sure you understand what the doctor tells you, don't hesitate to ask questions. If he is using too many technical terms, ask him to explain them. If he makes recommendations for treatment, follow them or else explore with him why you don't want to, or can't follow them. Don't just go home and say, "Well, the doctor said we should have some special test made, but I don't think he is right." If a doctor offers a recommendation that doesn't make sense to you, either ask for more explanation or seek an alternative opinion. If you think the doctor was wrong, ask yourself why you think so. If you come up with a sensible reason, seek someone else's opinion. This does not mean that you should run from doctor to doctor trying to find one who agrees with you; it does mean that if you have a legitimate question based on your knowledge or observation, it is your prerogative and responsibility to follow it up and seek either confirmation or disproof. Try not to be afraid that the professionals are judging you. Mostly they aren't, but even if they are, they aren't judging you any more than you are judging them. You feel that you are being weighed in the balance because you do feel responsible for your child and his behavior, but professional people who study retarded children generally have a good understanding of the reality of the problems.

The role of the psychologist is usually to measure the child's level of ability, determine his rate of mental growth, and provide information to parents about growth and development, management techniques, and education possibilities. Parents' questions are many: How retarded is my child? How rapidly is he progressing? What can we expect of him in the future? What school should he attend? Where will he fit? Intelligence tests will provide partial, although not complete, answers. Psychologists usually will use more than one test and space tests over a period of time; children are reevaluated from time to time so that the accuracy of measurement and the stability of the child's rate of growth can be checked. Accuracy in predicting the final mental maturity level improves as the child grows older and more of the mental development process has been completed. For most retarded children, prediction is fairly good for school-age children and is useful even before school age. The psychologist will assemble data about a child's ability patterns and observations about his behavior. On these data will be based recommendations for education, school placement, and home management. Also, when these data are interpreted to parents, they can be helped to know which parts of a child's behavior are probably the result of his constitutional structure and which parts may be the result of his life experience.

A school social worker usually acts as a go-between for home and school. She has been in the child's home, knows the family situation, and is aware of other problems the family has. She is in some ways responsible for helping parents with day-to-day problems and with providing information about other sources of aid — what facilities, for what problems, at what cost. She is often the interpreter of the school to the home and of the home to the school. Social workers in other agencies may define their roles differently, but most are concerned with family problems.

In the sphere of education, the retarded child's teacher can be a gold mine of information. Teachers are the experts on your child at school, as you are, or can be, experts on your child at home. They know how he handles competition in the group, how he gets attention, what he is learning, how he responds when angry or frightened, what interests him, and how long he can work at a given project. There are some differences between the child who wants to succeed because he is involved with the task and the child who wants to succeed because he wants praise. The motivation for personal approval is less mature than that for task completion. The teacher knows about the child's ability to be a group member, which requires sharing attention. Some children in a one-to-one situation may do well, but it may be a long while before they can function in a group. The teacher can describe how the child reacts to management, discipline, punishment; she knows something of his awareness and appreciation of other people. All children are self-centered; retarded children, as we have noted, stay self-centered longer and outgrow it at different rates. The teacher can make suggestions about what can be worked on at home and at school. If you seem to want suggestions, she is more likely to make them. She will also tell you about your child's level of understanding. Many times, it is easy for those living with a retarded child at home and not seeing him against the framework of the group to overrate his comprehension. You expect a response that the child can't make because he doesn't know what you mean.

Therefore, teachers have special opportunities to be of assistance to parents, but there are also some problems inherent in the teacher-parent working relationship. One problem lies in vocabulary-terminology. Teachers have been so steeped in their professional training that they sometimes forget that terms and concepts so obvious to them are unfamiliar to parents. The teacher who mentions Jimmy's "visual-perceptual defects" may not be communicating at all with his mother.

Or a teacher may cloak unpleasant truths in language that seems less threatening. Instead of saying that Tommy is selfish, a teacher may say, "He appears to be somewhat self-centered." If she means that he does not follow rules, she may put it this way: "He seems to be something of a nonconformist." The intent may be to avoid hurting the parent's feelings, but in the long run this may be a false kindness. There is also some unconscious rivalry between parents and teachers. People who are attracted to teaching as a career get satisfaction from working with children and seeing children make progress. Consequently, they may exaggerate what they see because they want to feel that they have been successful. If a child isn't doing too well, everyone may know this but no one can bear to say that the lack is in the child. So it often happens that, in this kind of situation, parents blame the teacher and the teacher blames the parents. It takes emotional maturity to be able to look at the facts objectively.

Some people have personal problems with authority relationships. If a squad car signals you over to the side of the road, what is your first reaction? "What did I do? Was I going too fast?" You feel guilty even before you know what the problem is. Perhaps he was just going to warn you of a detour ahead, but immediately you feel that you have done something wrong. Many parents approach a teacher-parent conference with this attitude — "What have I done wrong now?" They view teachers as authority figures. Some of this feeling is a throwback to the times when as children we were called to the principal's office.

Teachers and parents, however, can complement each other. Because the teacher sees the child against the background of the group, she can usefully compare him with his peers, describe his progress, his interests, his rate of learning, and his behavior controls. She is comparing him, not with normal children, which would not be fair, but with other retarded children. Parents, in turn, can give to the teacher their longitudinal view of the child. What has the past been like? They have watched him through measles, high fevers, convulsions, and hospital studies; they have watched him react to playmates and discipline. They can also keep the teacher up to date on the home scene. If there are things going on at home which are upsetting to the child, it will be helpful to the teacher to know about them. If the child's father is away on a business trip for a week, or if his mother is taking care of a couple of preschoolers while their parents are getting ready to move, he may very well show some different behavior in reaction to these changes.

Children don't always act the same way in different situations, and reports may vary. A parent may describe a child's behavior at home, and his teacher may describe his behavior at school, and you might not think they were talking about the same child. Why not? Because the school situation is not the home situation. At school, he is with a group, competing, wanting to succeed, having to stand on his own feet, and learning some lessons about taking turns, sharing, adapting. At home, conflicts may be handled differently since usually there wouldn't be a group of children of about the same age there. If a ten-year-old is picking on a six-year-old, it's quite natural for the parent to step in and say, "Hey, you're too big; leave him alone." Often teachers and parents are describing different situations.

Just as parents may feel that admitting a problem is a reflection on them, so may teachers. This is something for parents to think about when they go to teacher-parent conferences. If parents go to a conference fearing that they will be criticized, they won't dare talk about what really concerns them. If teachers have this same fear of being criticized, they, too, will avoid talking about problems, and the value of the conference is lost. If parents can bring up a problem that really concerns them, often teachers can be helpful.

Adequate information, for both teacher and parent, is important. If both participants know what the child's ability level is, they can shape their thinking more realistically. Planning must proceed on the basis of the best evidence available at the time. It is important that both teacher and parent see the child as a person, not an object. He has problems, but he also has assets, strong points, charms. Sometimes we focus so intensely on the retardation that we forget, for the moment, that the child has social traits, emotional traits, feelings, interests; that he has a whole life to lead, even though it is cut to different dimensions than the life we lead. We need to make a distinction in our discussions between the child's problems in academic learning, which in the long run may not affect his day-to-day life very much, and his inability to make progress in learning which does affect his day-to-day life — self-care, self-responsibility, and "good sense." This is one of the distinctions which separates the educable group from the trainable group, but not in a clear-cut way. It is a zigzag separation; some trainables show more common sense than we would expect, while some educables do not show good common-sense behavior. We need to look carefully at behavior in order not to be misled by a test score.

We must above all recognize that, in this field, there is no such thing as "an answer." When you say to the teacher, "What should I do?" you should not expect a clear-cut answer. You can expect help, thoughtfulness, interest, and some suggestions, but these will lead to an approximate solution. Some suggestions are right for some families, but not for others. Just knowing that a child is in a trainable class does not tell us what his family experiences in living with him. If a family chooses institutional care, this doesn't mean that the parents are lazy and want to get rid of the child. If the parents of another child don't choose institutional care, that doesn't necessarily mean they are unrealistic. Some situations are not solvable; some children cannot be in school. We have to consider not only the individual and his rights and needs, but the group and its rights and needs.

School is not the only place in which children learn. Parents can find many opportunities to broaden a child's experience. Because retarded children are so limited in their ability to generalize, they need as many specific experiences as can realistically be provided for them. It is also essential that children have some advance preparation for experiences, some understanding of what is going to happen, and some review of the event after it has occurred. Retardates must have help in acquiring meanings, and there are opportunities for parents here in giving directions, in offering choices, in using demonstrations and gestures to supplement the meanings of words. Make use of ideas such as "bigger," "smaller," "longer," "shorter," and directional words like "on top of," "in front of," "up," "down," "right," "left," as well as color names and number concepts.

When parents conscientiously try to build in their child a good basis for school experience, they also gain in their own understanding of him and his growth processes. Encouraging a child to do things for himself is a basic step; next comes encouraging him to do things for other people, to carry some share of responsibility in the family. As stressed earlier, children need to experience success if they are to show personality growth and emotional health. Praise, appreciation, and approval help to build strengths. Honesty is important. You cannot praise a child for something he didn't do and have him believe you. If you can't give him genuine praise for achievement, praise him for effort. We often miss chances to praise effort when it does not achieve full success; this is too bad because effort deserves praise. If you can't praise him for effort, don't praise him at all; turn your attention to the next time when he'll do better. Praise has to be real if it is to be a good motivator. It is important to prevent unnecessary failures and, when failures do occur, not to pay too much attention to them. When a child needs help, give it to him, but do so inconspicuously. Don't create issues which point out his inadequacies. Often, if there is time enough, he can do things for himself. It is your job to manage the situation so that there is time enough. Although we can govern children by being authoritarian and keeping them in line, our real aim is to help children, as far as possible, to be self-governing and to take responsibility for themselves. This means that the controls they develop must be in them, not in us. For children of limited capacity, we have to control situations to a greater extent, but we still want controls to be developing within the children.

Helping parents to help their children live more effectively is one of the goals of professional people. Parents, in turn, might set as one of their goals making themselves open and available to the help that is offered. Using help from professional people is a two-way street. Professionals can only give information, predictions, interpretations, and suggestions. It is the parents who have to put them to work in their own situations.

Parents should not try to feel like teachers, or act like social workers, or behave like psychologists. They should feel and act like parents. Children need parents who are loving, security-giving, consistent, strong, and concerned about the child's best welfare. They also need other people; there is a place for the professional view of a child and for professional evaluation of how he functions and what kinds of help he can use. The parental view and the professional view complementing each other can provide the best planning for the child.

11 SPECIAL EDUCATION

SPECIAL education began in the United States at the turn of this century when people in a few places started sifting children out of regular grades into subgroups for special attention. This was done chiefly because these children couldn't readily be tolerated in the regular grades. In a sense, then, there was a somewhat negative purpose at the beginning of special education. At that time, useful measures of intelligence had not been formulated, so the sifting could not be done on what we would now consider to be a sound diagnostic basis. Some of the reports of these earlier times were honest enough to indicate openly that behavioral problems were the major reason why a child was removed from his regular class. These early special education classes were, then, primarily "handling grounds" for children who were not manageable in the ordinary classroom. With the development of intelligence tests and the rapid expansion of their use, the selection of children for special subgroups could be made on the basis of a different comprehension of children's behavior — their measurable inability to keep up with the work in the regular class and the consequent development of problem behavior as a reaction to failure and frustration. Better recognition of the limitations of the children led to more positive purposes of the classes with more consideration of how these children could be helped to learn. People started asking what school could do to help these children function better, rather than just finding a way to remove them from regular classes so other children could function better. This was an important shift in thinking.

There were other problems, too, in the early 1900's. Mandatory education was not taken for granted, as it is now. The geographical distribution of the population was markedly different and communication and transportation media did little to facilitate quick exchange of information and experiments among educators. Curricula were bounded by the traditions of classical education. Research in child development and individual differences was in its scientific infancy. Over the intervening years, there have been many changes, related to population increases, urbanization, broadening concepts of what education can offer children. One element that affected special education in its early days, and still does, is the attitude of parents toward the school's desire to do something different with their child. Some parents took the view that their child could learn in a situation in which other children were learning, and, if he didn't learn, it was someone else's fault. They did not recognize in their child any basic lack of capacity to learn. Some parents did not accept the fact of retardation, and would not accept the concept of separating their child from the mainstream of education and placing him in a more specialized program. The schools, having a real need for some grouping procedures, sometimes reacted to this by trying to find ways to avoid the issue of defining and explaining mental retardation. Sometimes they presented special classes as specialized remedial classes or tutoring classes, thus skirting the issue of explaining retardation. This didn't work very well, either. The schools that tried to sell special classes as "remedial" usually got into deeper trouble, because they really weren't remedial, and they also needed classes which were genuinely remedial for other children. The schools that didn't face the real issue became less able to make realistic interpretations of retardation, less able to be useful to parents, and less able to make their special classes occupy a respectable place in the total program of the schools. A major factor in the change of attitude which is taking place is, I am sure, the work of parent associations in molding parent opinion. As parents insisted that they wanted to understand retardation better, it became easier for professionals to put their cards on the table. Schools, especially, were invited to explain special education.

Before we can define what special education for retarded children is like, we have to think of what the children themselves are like. Here it will be well to review some of the characteristics we've already noted in earlier chapters so that they can be seen as they relate to the classroom. A basic characteristic of retarded children is their slower than average rate of mental development. Educationally, this means that the child is not mature enough to adapt to the program which children of his age follow. His slower rate of mental growth has other implications for the learning situation. He may be restless and easily distracted in the classroom, partly because he is not interested in the material, which is too difficult for him, and partly because he is restless and distractible in any setting. His restlessness is a basic trait, accentuated by the unsuitability of the material, but not created by it. When he has repeated experiences of failure in the normal classroom, he is likely to react with discouragement, even less interest, and loss of motivation. It doesn't take long for a child to become aware of failure. Very quickly, we have some secondary problems developing. A retarded child in a normal classroom will probably become increasingly disinterested in school; soon he will deny ever having been interested or ever having wanted

MENTALLY RETARDED CHILDREN

to succeed, and he will be saying, "I hate it, I hate the teacher, I don't want to learn it."⟩

Retarded children show their need for special programming in other ways. At early school ages, they are less mature and less proficient in motor skills of all kinds. They take longer to learn to throw or catch a ball, to roller-skate, to jump rope. They are clumsy in fine motor coordination; eight- and nine-year-old trainables have great difficulty in cutting with a scissors—a task which preschool children can do crudely before the age of three and with some finesse by kindergarten age. Or take coloring. Crayons are a familiar toy for parents to get children—inexpensive, easily accessible, requiring only paper to go with them, and providing a quiet activity. But most retarded children cannot enjoy crayons at preschool levels. Much frustration and criticism are related to them: "Stay inside the lines," "Don't color like that," "Don't make the boy's hair blue." When these children come to school, it's useful to hide the crayons, get out the finger paints, and say, in effect, "Go ahead, hate everybody; smear this stuff all over this wet paper," because this is one purpose of finger painting—to help neutralize some of the negative effects of earlier failures. There are general language disabilities not only in articulation, but also in maturity of content, language structure, vocabulary, and interest level. Because of short attention spans, projects have to be limited in length as well as graded in difficulty. Retardates are socially less adept. They are more self-centered and less aware of other people. Usually they have had less social experience because they haven't been able to play successfully with other children, so this experience has not been fostered by their parents. They don't know how to get along as a member of a group. They may have constant, or nearly constant, need for individual attention. They have trouble understanding, remembering, and following the rules for the simplest games. Repetition is necessary in all sorts of experiences. For instance, retardates must be exposed to concrete learning, with the same content, in many different ways, over and over again, before it becomes meaningful and useful to them. With milder degrees of retardation, the number of repetitions may be fewer, but in comparison with normal children, even the more competent of the educable retarded need much repetition.

The individual differences that exist among retarded children must be taken into account. Even retardates of the same mental age may be markedly different in their skills. The child more competent with speech certainly has more chances for social rewards and fewer instances of frustration in the communication process; he will also get along better in school than the child severely handicapped in speech. The child (often one who falls in the organically damaged group) who has special problems in visual-perceptual-motor organization so that he can't accurately see relationships between parts and wholes, or make accurate size and shape discriminations, will more likely have trouble with reading than a similar ability youngster who doesn't happen to have this kind of problem. The child who can't sustain attention, the "flickering" child, has a learning handicap different from, but as significant as, that of a speech handicap or a perceptual defect.

There have been many approaches to special education. No one knows for sure what educational method or technique will be right for every child. The best we can do is to make approximations based on knowledge, judgment, and study of individual children. One approach has been academic force-feeding — drill and more drill. This may be useful and appropriate for children older than ten, but at earlier ages, I think it contributes negatively to good adjustment and developmental progress. Since this has been a frequent educational approach, this is what many parents expect special education to be — a program in which, no matter what the child is like, somebody will teach him, by whatever method is necessary, the things we associate with school, that is, reading, writing, arithmetic. Most of you who have trainable children have come to recognize that this is not a good use of time for most of your children. Some of you who are parents of educable children are beginning to realize that even though the IQ score says "educable," reading is not going to be one of your child's major achievements.

Another approach is to emphasize the child — his development and his total adjustment, not just his academic learning. There are three key aspects to this approach. The first and most important is the teacher. The live, human, sensible, well-adjusted, interested teacher is essential. The next key is progress. Concern is not so much with rate or destination as with motion and direction. Is the child changing? Does he do things differently? For some children, progress is learning to defend their rights; perhaps, up to now, they have stood helplessly by while someone else exploited them. For others, it is progress if they learn more self-control. The same goals are not suitable for every child; they must be individualized. Consequently, the third key is the individual, tailor-made program, which tries to see what problems are most significant to each child and what can be done to solve or lessen them. This approach stresses general learning and experience, chiefly on a concrete level, which will help each child carry his potential as far as he can. Attention is focused on giving the children as many experiences as possible — people, events, pictures, movies, music, books, projects, visitors. Everything goes into this "corn popper" of life experiences for children to sample. Given the opportunity to learn, and the materials with which to learn, the child will make use of them when he can. When this point arrives, the alert teacher sees it and feeds more content and direction into the learning process. Then the child's progress becomes more satisfying to him and his future progress is enhanced by his success. The goal is not to have the teacher say, "I taught thirteen children how to spell ten words today," but rather, "Thirteen children had a good day in school; they all learned something and had some good experiences, which we will build on tomorrow." It is a matter of where we put the focus — on the content or on the child.

This is the approach of the Sheltering Arms. Suppose you were a visitor to this school. What would you see?

Approaching the school on the curving drive which parallels the Mississippi River, you would first see a sign, "Sheltering Arms, A Day School and Research Program for Mentally Retarded Children." (Not everyone approves of the wording; should it say "for Handicapped Children?" Or "for Exceptional Children?" We think not.) Driving in through the stone gate, you have an immediate impression of spaciousness; there are lots of trees, twelve acres of land, clusters of playground equipment — swings, a merry-go-round, things to climb on, a slide, a buck-about safe substitute for a teeter-totter. If it's playtime when you arrive, you'll drive with care because there are children all over the place, riding bicycles or tricycles, pulling someone else in a wagon, roller skating, jumping rope, and just running around. If you stop in front of the main building, you'll see half a dozen youngsters sitting on the steps; not all retarded children enjoy vigorous physical play. Probably one or more of the bicycle riders or step sitters will come up to your car and ask you if you're going to visit school, or if you're coming to a meeting, or if the child with you is going to be a "new kid" in school. The outgoing, friendly, socially aware, and responsive behavior of the children will be something you notice quickly. You'll see five or six adults scattered around supervising the play, monitoring the taking of turns, encouraging effort and learning, and often just conversing with the children.

The main building is old: it was built around 1910 as an

orphanage. Since then, it has gone through a couple of meta-morphoses — first serving as a hospital for the treatment of poliomyelitis from about 1941 to 1955, and then being further modified to begin its career as a school. Classrooms for the younger groups are large, high-ceilinged, many-windowed, permitting varied activities to be pursued at the same time. Classrooms for the two older groups are smaller, but are supplemented by adjacent additional small rooms permitting subdivision of the class into smaller groups for different activities. The "new" building, Gregg Hall, first used in the 1968–69 school year, houses a gymnasium on the upper level and an auditorium on the lower level. It is connected to the main building by a walk-through ramp. Your guide (and you'll need one if it's your first visit) will tell you that currently sixty-five children attend school here; that there are six classes — three for trainables, three for educables — with a range in age of pupils from six to fourteen. You'll learn that each of the teachers of the four younger classes has a classroom assistant, and that the teachers of the two older groups (ages eleven to fourteen) share an assistant. As you visit classes and note that there are additional adults in some of the rooms, you will learn that some of them are volunteers, some are college students, some are high school volunteers from neighboring Breck School who choose to use part of their study periods to help at Sheltering Arms.

What's going on in the classrooms? Different things, of course, for the differing age and ability levels, but all the classroom groups reflect the philosophy that school is for children; that children are people; that broad and varied experiences contribute to learning; that acceptance, liking, security, companionship, and activity are essential components of helping retarded children learn to live at their optimum level; that motivation and interests grow out of successes (and also out of some failures, and some repeated trials); that no two children are alike.

In the young trainable group, the average age may be about seven and a half, the average IQ about 46. The ten children in the group include two or three Mongoloids, with the others representing some instances of known organic damage and some "unknown causation." Speech skills are at a low level; probably a couple of the children talk very little or not at all, and for most of them, speech is very defective. Some of the school day is quite individualized in this room, while some of it is fairly structured. If you visit at an "individualized" time, a couple of youngsters are likely to be playing favorite records, perhaps singing along with the ones they know. Two or three others are engaged in dramatic play in the dollhouse corner. One child seems to be paying no attention to the group; he is sitting at a table by himself, building with lego blocks. The speech therapist has just taken another child out of the room for some individual speech work. The other three are sitting at the table working puzzles. What's the teacher doing? What's the classroom assistant doing? They're busily occupied giving help wherever needed, reminding the children of some of the basic rules ("He's using that puzzle, now, Freddy; why don't you take the snowman one?" "Move your chair this way, Sally, you aren't leaving him any room") and exercising preventive discipline — seeing, in advance of their actual appearance, the interpersonal conflicts, the hitting, biting, scratching that go with the beginnings of socialization. Jimmy tears up the picture that David just finished, before anyone can stop him. David is angry, crying, and trying to beat up Jimmy. It's time for the teacher to be there, quickly, interpreting feelings and property rights ("That was his picture, Jimmy; he's mad at you for tearing it," and, to David, "We can get you some more paper; would you like to make another one?").

A more structured time of day might find this group gathered around the work table (no individual desks for this class) with dittoed worksheets involving color learning or matching shapes. If they've been listening to a story about "The Gingerbread Boy," perhaps this is the day they are going to make cookies. The gingerbread boy cookie cutter is in readiness; all the children have a turn to stir the cookie dough, and the whole process is observed and talked about. A committee of two or three accompany the teacher to put the cookies in the oven; a different committee helps take them out. Taking turns, waiting a turn, seeing a project through from beginning to end, building in some concrete information about food, its preparation, the sequence from raw material to product, the importance of washing hands, the caution needed in dealing with stoves and hot ovens — all this is useful learning.

You might expect that the young educable group, in contrast to the beginning trainable group, would be at work on much more academic pursuits. Remember, however, that the "average" six-year-old educable, with an IQ in the mid-sixties, is just about four, mentally. He's not yet ready for reading, although he's more mature intellectually than the typical six-year-old beginning trainable with an IQ in the 40's and a mental age of under three. In the young educable group, the projects are not too startlingly different, although they are carried out at a slightly higher level, and usually with slightly less individual help from the teacher or classroom assistant. Work periods find the twelve-member group often broken up into smaller groups, with the teacher working with one four-member group on reading readiness, the classroom assistant working with another group on similar material, and perhaps a volunteer helping the remaining four with a game, a library period, or an extra gym practice session of somersaults or roller skating. The reading readiness, in fact, the general readiness program, does not differ too much from what goes on in the younger trainable groups, except that it progresses faster and goes further. Discriminating forms and shapes, learning colors, number concepts, and letters, recognizing words, beginning to print, draw, paint, and color, working puzzles, playing games, practicing language through morning meeting discussions, having social experience through free play time and structured classroom time — all these things are woven into the daily program.

As the children grow older, structure is increased and demands for conformity are heightened. In the older trainable group — ages eleven to fourteen — the semi-academic demands have to be very much individualized, because at these ages the differences in learning capacity between the lower and higher trainable ability levels are conspicuous. Some children are, in fact, using workbooks, doing some easy reading, making use of beginning addition and subtraction skills, while others, less competent intellectually, are still working at pre-academic levels. There is a lot of concrete experience learning, and considerable emphasis on "growing up" behavior. Children introduce themselves to visiting groups. There are many projects related to daily living, practical skills, awareness of the world around them. Science means planting seeds and watching them grow, collecting pictures and making books to demonstrate "seeds that we eat," weather reporting, keeping temperature records. Arithmetic means continuing stress on counting (simple for normal children, not simple at all for the trainable retarded), use of numbers, ideas about money. Language and communication mean not only general verbal communication, but training in the use of the telephone, through a training kit made available by the Northwestern Bell Telephone Company, for dialing, answering, message taking. Children are taught how to answer, and what to say, when their parents are not at home; there is an emphasis on safety as well as on communication.

The older educable group, meanwhile, is being prepared for transition to the city's special education program at the junior high school level. Independent study skills are important to develop. Again, achievement level varies considerably — from about a first-grade reading level up to a fifth-grade reading level. A group arithmetic lesson may be twenty addition and subtraction problems on the blackboard, at varying levels of difficulty; children take turns coming to the board, selecting a problem to do, and solving it, while the group watches, approves success, points out errors. The gym period is combined for the two older groups, trainable and educable. Much stress here is on following directions, as well as on the motor skills required. Relay races, cage ball, volleyball, shooting baskets are some of the familiar activities. Calisthenics involve imitation, following directions. Practice with situps often involves teaming two children as partners. Social learning continues to be a major purpose.

We see, in the progression of children from the beginning groups, both trainable and educable, through the middle groups (roughly ages nine to eleven), to the older groups, a gradual shift in emphasis: in the early days stress is placed on trying to recognize and understand the developmental levels and emotional problems of individual children, and to give them individualized expectations and handling; then there is an interim period when demands for conformity are stepped up and structure is increased; finally, for the two older classes, although the school "work" is still individualized, the social and behavioral requirements are tightened and heightened. If retarded children are to be able to live in the community, at any level, they must acquire behavior traits which are acceptable, and some skills, at some level, to occupy them, give them a feeling of usefulness and "belonging to the world." They must be helped to know, behaviorally if not intellectually, how to observe the rights of others.

The whole school shares in many activities, and younger children admire and look up to older children, and anticipate the day when they, in turn, will become "the big kids." Older children are reminded that they set examples for younger ones. Responsibility-taking increases. Even the youngest groups send messengers around the building to report attendance — to the kitchen, to the social worker's office, to the school clerk's office — but the beginners often go in pairs, with the slightly older child being "in charge" of the errand while the brand-new child is learning. Educational movies find the whole school in the auditorium, where, again, younger children are exposed to the more mature behavior of the older groups. Individual misbehavior generally brings exclusion from the event. Sing-alongs, special entertainment programs brought to the school by various community groups, recognition ceremonies for retiring staff members, and the weekly chapel service provide extensive practice with social behavior. Since Sheltering Arms is, in a sense, a demonstration school, we have many groups of visitors; the field trips of these groups to the school also provide social practice as students from various colleges and schools of nursing and interested community organizations and "visiting firemen" come to observe the program. A music volunteer works weekly with the two older classes; an art volunteer may spend half a day a week on special art projects. Parent committees conduct a Boys' Club and Girls' Club program one day a week, as a post-lunch activity. The two older classes constitute the school choir and sing each week at chapel; sometimes an individual child is the soloist. There are numerous field trips, sometimes for a single class, sometimes for the whole school — to Como Park, to the Museum of Natural History, to see the circus unload. Every other year the two older classes visit the State Capitol. Children bring things or news of interest for the morning meeting of each class; what they say ranges from the hard-to-understand news of the beginning trainable — "It's snowing today" — to pictures or clippings from newspapers which an older educable child might bring.

What are the teachers like? They share a background of training in special education, but also bring a variety of other backgrounds — teaching physical education, business education, nursery school, regular elementary grades, for example. Teachers teach through the use of themselves, their own personalities, interests, concern with children's growth and learning. We once did a small study to try to assess some of the traits of teachers, giving our teachers and some of our volunteers a battery of tests of attitude, ability, personality, and interests. While the number of participants was too small to lead to any definitive conclusions, it did appear that an outstanding characteristic of successful teachers of retarded children is a strong interest in individuals. On the interest test, for example, our staff people scored high for vocational interest in psychology, social work, and medicine, and scored lower for vocational interest in "teaching" per se. Our classroom assistants are not professionally trained, and are selected primarily on the basis of these same personality traits. Interest in and liking for children, nondefensiveness as people, a sense of humor, imagination, and an ability to appreciate the growth and learning processes in children are the essential ingredients. Of course, as they work with teachers, they acquire a great deal of in-service training and gradually become more and more expert in their own right.

Sheltering Arms differs from some other special education settings, we believe, in focusing on the total development of the child as a person rather than, more narrowly, on academic learning only, or primarily. It also differs in the emphasis it gives to the importance of work with parents. We place the highest value on openness of communication, honesty of interpretation, and trying to help parents understand the larger picture of retardation, beyond the ability level and problems of their own child. We are concerned with helping children grow up in every area, and with equipping them as well as they can be equipped to function, to belong, to contribute, and to enjoy their total lives. We sacrifice, I suspect, some of the adult comfort which may prevail in settings in which children are, at early ages, overcontrolled and overdirected by adults; this temporary sacrifice is more than compensated for by the longer range, and, we believe, more valuable outcome of seeing children learn to be self-controlled and self-directive in situations suited to their ability levels.

You who are parents of a retarded child are likely to be extremely anxious about the school situation he will be in. You are first of all anxious that he be *in* a school. Then you are anxious that this school be just exactly right for him. Things don't always go smoothly for your normal children at school. They run into teachers they don't like, or who don't seem to like them; they don't always get the highest grades. Even so, you tend to accept the fact that school for your normal children will, like all of life, have its ups and downs. You trust your normal children to have some stamina and ability to learn to manage some school problems for themselves. You may even express this to the child sometimes. If he doesn't get his homework done and the teacher gives him an extra assignment, you may say, "It's what you deserve. Next time maybe you'll remember to get it done on time."

It's very hard to have this attitude toward your retarded child. Where he is concerned, you are likely to be much more "touchy." You want perfection in his school and are critical of its lack. Subconsciously, perhaps, you want a school that can fix everything, can make the child be normal. You recognize that other retarded children will also be attending his school, but inwardly you don't quite like this and secretly you may feel that those other children are a lot worse than yours.

Your child is going to be different, and it must be the school's fault if he isn't rapidly becoming different. You want your child to be accepted by others, and you say that social experience is important, yet you are worried and upset if you hear that another child hit him. You think, "Why didn't the teacher interfere?" Many times you cannot believe that he is disobedient at school because he is never disobedient at home. You may not realize, without some careful review, the extent to which you don't ask him to be obedient at home. If you don't make demands of him, he isn't being disobedient by not fulfilling them. If your child is difficult at home, you worry about whether he is also difficult in school, and if he is in danger of being excluded. This fear makes your relationship to the school complex. You perhaps resent the school somewhat because of the power it has over your child's life and, indirectly, over yours. At the same time you are anxious to please the school, to be cooperative. There may be some feeling that if you're cooperative enough, this will compensate for problems the child may be presenting.

There is another side of the coin. You do know that your child is different from normal. You often find him hard to live with, or too dependent, or too hyperactive, and you get frustrated and discouraged. You know that you swing from being indulgent and sympathetic to being pressuring and severe, and back again. You know that in school, whatever school he is in, he has a chance for companionship, learning experiences, stimulation, and self-help skills. You really appreciate this, and you appreciate what the teacher is doing. You do recognize too, most of you, that the most essential goal for any person, including the retardate, is learning to live, not just learning to learn for the sake of learning or learning to do for the sake of doing. And you are deeply grateful when the school helps you in helping your retarded child to learn to live with himself and with others.

12 FAMILY LIVING AND ITS PROBLEMS

LIVING in families involves many problems — establishing rules and enforcing discipline, balancing family responsibilities, using leisure time, maintaining relations with grandparents and other relatives. Let's consider the special implications such problems have when there is a retarded child in the family.

In talking about families, we first must think about the ways in which families differ from each other. A conspicuous difference lies in values — what one family stresses may not be important at all to another family; how one family lives may not suit another at all. Any group of parents of mentally retarded children may well have only one thing in common — they all have mentally retarded children. What may be a practical solution to the problem of retardation for one family may not work for another. There are differences in "life style"; there are differences in the way family members adjust to individual differences. Some people married to each other are highly compatible and like the same things. Some people married to each other who love each other very much are highly noncompatible in some ways and like different things. So there are conflicts: One partner likes to go to the movies and the other doesn't; one likes picnics and the other detests the company of ants. One likes to play cards and the other would prefer to dance. How do people react? Do they fight? Do they take turns? Do they compromise, do they go in separate directions, or do they stay home and do nothing if they can't come to an agreement? These things affect the way families live. One parent says, "I can't stand going to the Art Institute, and that's all there is to it," to which his partner responds, "Well, dear, we won't go to the Art Institute," and that *is* all there is to it! Compare this with the couple which compromises, with one partner saying, "Okay, you like art and I don't; I'll go to the Art Institute with you tomorrow if you will go to the baseball game with me Tuesday." There are differences between domination, compromise, and the whole range of styles of living which they suggest.

There are also differences between the seclusive family and the expansive family. The retarded child is somewhat more likely to live in a seclusive family because there are so many ways in which retardation changes family life. The seclusive family shuts out the rest of the world. Perhaps the parents don't go to church because they can't take their retarded child. Or perhaps one goes and the other stays home, or they take turns. They work out different ways of managing, and often the ways that work shut them out from normal family patterns. At the other end of the distribution there is the expansive family, and of course there are all kinds of stages in between. The expansive family is "hail-fellow-well-met." Its front door is always unlocked, and generally open; kids from the neighborhood stream through the house; people are casually entertained in the summertime — the family decides to have a backyard barbecue, buys ten pounds of hamburger, and invites the whole neighborhood. This is quite a contrast to the seclusive family, which lives to itself, in which the children have family loyalty first and their friends come second. In an expansive family, the friends are right there on a par with the family; everybody is a pal. In some families the members are very close to each other and care deeply about each other, yet everyone has a lot of freedom and independence. The children at an early age go in their own directions. They belong to clubs, they go to meetings, they visit around the neighborhood, they spend weekends with their friends, and they come home occasionally to eat and sleep and pick up clean clothes. Then there are families in which visiting and "neighboring" are very, very restricted.

Another value difference concerns the role of work. There are families in which both parents are employed; families in which only one parent is employed. Some families have two parents employed on two jobs apiece, and some families have one parent employed on two jobs. There are different roles within the family situation. Who looks after the children? Who takes responsibility for decisions? Who supervises? Who makes the rules? When we talk about jobs, we must also talk about job satisfactions. There are families in which people like their work, and other families in which going to work is the worst part of the day. You have to go and put in your time because this is what you get paid for and this is how you live, but perhaps you hate every minute of it. This is a different attitude to reflect at home than that of liking one's job. Attitudes toward jobs range from liking to toleration to dislike and resentment.

Related to jobs is the question of who handles the money of the family. Democracy or autocracy, sharing or an allowance for one partner? Is it the husband who says, "Give me five dollars to cover my lunches?" or the wife who says, "Give me the grocery money or we don't eat tonight"? Is there tension about money? What are the checks and balances of dealing with the budget? Is there a real financial crisis? It is ridiculous to talk about psychological values when worry about the basic necessities of life is an overriding family concern.

What is the general family attitude toward raising children? Are the parents dictators? "Sit down! . . . Well, because I said so." "I won't." "Sit down or I'll spank you. Sit down and stay put." "What if I don't?" "Go to your room." Is authority heavily imposed, physically imposed, or is there a more democratic atmosphere? "Sit down." "I don't want to." "Why not?" 'Because I have to go to the bathroom." There are times when a child has a point and ought to be listened to. The strictly authoritarian parent sometimes lives to regret his attitude.

Some homes are adult-centered: there may be two parents and one child, or two parents, grown-up children, and one younger child. What happens here? The one child is exposed to adult ways of behaving and living, adult friends, sociability, and recreation, as contrasted with the child-centered home where there may be four or five, or seven or eight, children. If there are that many children, it is not an adult-centered home — it is child-centered. When are the kids hungry? That's when you feed them. What do you feed them? What you can afford, for six or eight or more. More often hot dogs than tenderloins.

There is the matter of how responsibilities are divided in the family. What jobs do the children have? What does the father do? Is he the kind of father who, if the door falls off, will put it back on its hinges? Will he change the baby's diapers or wash the dishes or get the dinner? Fathers see the paternal role in many different ways. Who's to say which is right and which is wrong? It depends on the people and their relationships with each other. Still, these things make differences in how families live. Are the children supposed to make their beds? *Do* they make their beds? Do they see this as something reasonably expected of them, or as something they should get paid a quarter for doing? Families define differently the roles, the responsibilities, of children and of parents.

With these differences among families in mind, we can look

at some of the special problems having a retarded child is likely to entail in family living. Problems of management relate to efforts to instill conformity and responsibility. "Pick up your toys," "Stop fighting," "Don't hit him," "Go to the bathroom," "Get undressed," "Take your bath." How does the child react to parental direction and guidance? Does he resist, rebel, refuse, understand, conform? Is he cooperative, resentful, angry, or even perhaps unable to respond? We have to look at many possibilities before we can define what the problem is and decide how to handle it.

In most families in which there is a retarded child there are normal children as well. You say, "Dick, pick up your toys," and he does, because he has been well taught and his IQ is 110. Then you say, "Jimmy, pick up your toys," and Jimmy doesn't make a move. His IQ is 58, and you have tried to teach him. Even so, he hasn't learned, so he doesn't pick up his toys. Here is a management problem which affects the children's relationships with each other. How do you handle this?

From watching many parents try to cope with a problem like this, I would judge that the predominant parental reaction is overprotection. If the retarded child can't, won't, or doesn't want to do something, the most typical reaction of parents is to do it for him. If something seems to be hard for him to learn, the parent feels it easier to do it for him than to teach him. This is a "cardinal sin" of parents — failing to help the child become self-reliant. It surely isn't easy. I don't mean that you can do it with perfect confidence or with perfect success. How do you know what to expect? Can he make his own bed? Well, no, not perfectly, but neither does your normal eight-year-old. Can he wash the dishes? Can he rake the yard? Children should not be permitted to destroy things in their clumsy efforts to learn, but they do need to learn to take responsibility as a member of a family, just as

113

you try to teach your normal children to do. How do you divide things up among the children? What's fair? Normal children need to have their rights considered, too.

There are management problems in the neighborhood too. Some lucky families have enough space between their house and the next house to avoid many difficulties. Some are lucky enough to have the kind of retarded child who does not create neighborhood problems. Some retarded children, because of judgment defects and a need to be active, set fire to garages, throw stones through windows, turn on hoses, tear up flowers, start fights with other children. As a parent, how do you re-act to this? No matter how fair-minded you try to be, I suspect that many of you react with a counter-accusation: "Well, sup-pose he did—your Tommy broke a window in our house once!" This is natural and human but not very constructive. You'll do better if you can say, "Well, he did, and his be-havior is our responsibility. We do have to manage him bet-ter if he is to live in the community." This is hard. It takes an extra margin of emotional maturity to be objective enough to recognize your retarded child's liabilities and his lack of control, and still to love him and want to help him to become more competent.

How do you react to such problems? Many of you are still "waiting to see." You can't believe yet the limitations under which your child will operate all of his life. This is under-standable, but unrealistic. In a general way we know what a child's ability level means for his future. I think it is im-portant for professional people to help parents make long-range plans. When you hide behind the thought that he'll be different when he is older, this is postponing the problem. It won't help a bit when the "later" becomes the present. (Chapter 14, devoted to planning for the future, will return to this theme.)

There are some things not to do about problems. One of

the most important is not to deny a problem's existence. It won't go away just by pretending it isn't there. Another is not to make excuses. You might say, "He doesn't hang up his clothing." Then the next logical thought is "What should I do about it?" When you simply take the responsibility and say it is your fault, you excuse yourself from finding a solution which helps the child.

What can we do about problems of management? Look at them; don't run away from them. Analyze them, think about them, look at the child's day-to-day life experience through his eyes, not through yours. What does he get out of living? What is rewarding to him? What is frustrating? What is disappointing? What does he like to do? What does he want to work at? What does he reject? Almost any time that we give a child an adult-type job to do, he will do it. We miss first opportunities to help children learn when they are too little to be really helpful but are very eager to try. Later, when we want them to be helpful, they have gotten tired of the idea. From early years too we can help them acquire controls. Retarded youngsters are quite concrete in their ideas and thinking, but they can learn, at least on a basis of habit, some generalizations. The retarded child who says to another one who is attacking him, "Cut that out. I don't want to fight," is practicing the principle of "preventive fighting." This kind of control must be encouraged if children of limited ability are to live in the world. Try to avoid overprotection. Help your retarded child in every way you can to develop independent behavior. Help him be motivated, to want to do things, but keep aspirations within what is reasonable. Pay attention to your own work attitudes. Many retarded children are going to spend their lives doing things that many normal people don't want to do. If such children see you resenting it when you wash dishes, mop floors, or make beds, they may come to feel that these tasks are unworthy, whereas for the retarded, these

115

may be the very tasks which will provide the greatest sources of satisfaction, ego strength, and feelings of achievement. Nothing that needs to be done is unworthy of being done, and this attitude can be exemplified in the home by parents. Appreciate the things the child does which are good. We are all too inclined to take good behavior for granted, and to pounce on bad behavior. Approval for good behavior is the most effective way of making sure that it will be repeated by the child.

Some problems of management will be eased if you can enlist the support of your normal sons and daughters in setting an example and in helping establish good habits in their retarded brother or sister. I have found that many teen-agers of normal ability have good attitudes and good answers about retardation in a member of their family. Many of them feel that having a retarded brother or sister has made them develop strength, understanding, tolerance, patience, and fortitude they might not have had otherwise. They admit to being irritated, embarrassed, annoyed, or angry at their retarded brother or sister occasionally and to feeling guilty if they show their feelings too much. They admit to deliberately letting the retarded ones win at games, but they feel guilty if they don't play games with them sometimes. The general picture as I have seen it is of a pretty well-adjusted group of adolescents, but not a contented group. There is a lot of conflict involved. Conflict, however, is of course a part of life. They are ambivalent; they feel protective, but they also feel resentful. One of the things they often mention is public embarrassment. This is something to which you parents might give special thought—trying to avoid ways in which your normal youngsters are publicly embarrassed. Interpreting the retarded child to the normal children is important from the earliest days, in the same gradual way you interpret attitudes toward education, religion, and sex. It is above all important not to expect the normal child to achieve too much, just as it is important not to expect too little from the retarded child.

An important part of family life revolves around the use of leisure and vacation time. People look forward to summer. The pace is a little more relaxed; there aren't so many people in the family who have to be on tight time schedules; entertaining and socializing are informal, backyard affairs. Even though the children are out of school, there are in most neighborhoods quite a few organized and semi-organized activities for them — summer school, Little League, park board and library activities, day camp, or regular camp. Meals can be informal, often outdoors; clothing can be informal and the laundry is an easier chore. Evenings are longer, and it is too light too late to worry about a strict bedtime hour for the children. Maybe there is a vacation trip in the offing to a cottage or resort, or a camping trip. The weeks of summer beckon invitingly; the pressures ease.

To parents with a retarded child, however, the weeks of summer can look very long. During the school year, the child is quite programmed — early bus, school all day, home in late afternoon. Weekends present a few more problems, but they usually get filled with shopping, routine chores, visits, church. Christmas and spring school vacations present still more problems. Most parents enjoy the first part of school vacation more than the last part. They are generally happy to have school resume.

Summer brings not only the problem of keeping the retarded child, as well as other children, busy for an extended period, while maintaining peace in the neighborhood, but also frequent or occasional disruption of routine in the form of visits to other people or from other people. You probably see many friends and relatives over the summer whom you don't see the rest of the year. So summer means that you will have two responsibilities you don't have, to the same degree

117

at least, during the rest of the year—planning activities and coping with the attitudes and feelings of visitors or hosts.

There is one good basic principle to remember. Children who have something to do get into less trouble than those who don't have something to do. Keeping children busy involves planning and preparation which admittedly takes time and energy. But it also takes time and energy to cope with the misbehavior, quarreling, disobedience, and irritability likely to occur when children are bored. Not that it's an all or none choice—you can do a little planning and have some problems, or no planning and have many problems, or a lot of planning and still have a few problems. Perhaps we can't entirely avoid the problems, but undoubtedly planning activities does help.

Family circumstances modify the situation. People with a summer cottage two miles from the nearest neighbors in which they spend the weeks from June till September are in a very different situation from that of those who stay in the city. People with a good park program nearby have an advantage over those without such a program. People with cooperative, understanding neighbors have different problems from those whose neighbors are critical, angry, or hostile. These situational factors make a difference in what you can do. Maybe you can't change your situation, but you can make the best of what it does offer.

Agencies can offer help. There may be day camping programs for retarded children. The camp experience doesn't have to end at the close of the session, either. You can take activities which the camp has introduced and build on these through the rest of the summer—crafts, sports, games, collections; perhaps even companions can be found at camp whom the retarded child can invite to his home from time to time. There are resident camping opportunities, especially worth considering if your family vacation plans are such that it isn't really suitable to take your retarded child with you. This is often the case, and it doesn't mean that your plans are wrong; it only means that you need to make a different plan for the retarded child. There are some advantages in the retarded child having a separate vacation, both for him and for the rest of the family. Whether he feels left out or not depends much on how you present the plan to him, and whether you feel that you're leaving him out or simply providing him with a better vacation. If you feel guilty about not taking him with you, he will be more likely to feel left out.

There are other things to do at home. You can create a special occasion on one day of the week — an excursion, something to look forward to, think about, and get ready to do. This is what schools do with special events: First, they prepare for them, then they have them, then they review them. When the occasion is over, you come back, talk about it; this helps make the child's learning more meaningful and, from the practical point of view, stretches out the effect. It might be a trip to the zoo, a day at the park, a picnic, a short trip, a visit to some interesting industry that provides public tours (depending on how well your child can be trusted to behave). Children usually will like things that you indicate are likable, so this gives you a chance to do something that interests you, too. It doesn't have to take a full day. It could be going swimming at a new place, or eating at a drive-in — anything that breaks the routine and makes the day feel special. If something interferes with carrying out the plan (it turns out to be too hot, or someone is sick) have some alternate ideas in mind. Sort rummage for the next rummage sale, match buttons, make scrapbooks, or clean the attic. If an activity seems to be out of the ordinary, even if it is work, often children will see it as fun instead.

When visitors are expected, it's important to include the retarded child in your planning. Often retarded children don't

119

adjust well to changes in routine; they need to know what to expect. If your child needs to adapt to sleeping on a cot in his brother's room, some explanation and probably also some practice are indicated. If you are going on a trip, the same principle applies — advance preparation, explanation, practice. Plan games for him to play in the car, have dampened face cloths and treats at hand, rotate seating arrangements, take short, frequent breaks.

Summer school may be helpful with some educable children who are already well motivated for learning. If a child needs, and can profit from, individual speech therapy, summer may be a good time to provide it.

Then there are days when you are at home, and there's nothing special to do. If your retarded child plays outdoors, you do need to supervise him. Supervision does not necessarily mean constant attention, but it does mean knowing where the child is, with whom he is, and depending on his general reliability, some checking on what is going on. He may be fine playing with one other child, but if a third one wanders onto the scene, trouble can start. You can't control how many children play together in a neighborhood situation, but you can keep an eye on it. In free play, impulsiveness, failure to foresee consequences of behavior, and lack of judgment are traits of children that can lead to a sudden crisis. For most educables in the eleven to fourteen age bracket, going to the nearby park will be all right. For some, it wouldn't be. For some, having a brother or sister along might make it all right; for others, this might make it worse. You have to know your own child to make some of these judgments. It is certainly better for a retarded child to spend one happy hour with other children than try to spend two which may end in tears.

There is likely to be some opportunity or need to explain your child to relatives or friends who don't see him often.

What other people need to know depends partly on who they are and how close you are to them. How well you can explain depends heavily on how accepting you truly are of the facts and the realities of your child's situation. Trying to make an explanation is probably good for you, if you will listen to yourself. You may be tempted to say, "Dick is in a trainable class, but of course he is really brighter than that," or "Susie is in a special education class, but we don't think she is really retarded," or "Don is a brain-injured child; he is in a special class with retarded children, but he's really brain-injured, not retarded." If you hear yourself saying things like these, stop and start over. A brain-injured child may be just as truly mentally retarded as a child whose retardation happened because of some other cause. Keep in mind that how you describe the problem will determine to a large extent how other people will react.

It is usually easier to explain a trainable child than an educable child because his defects are more conspicuous. They show up at an early age and are likely to be more extensive; he is more likely to have poor speech and poor coordination, to be more "visibly" retarded. The educable child, unless he also has a speech handicap, a seizure problem, or a conspicuous behavior problem, is less likely to be identified early and may not be diagnosed as retarded until after he is in school. People will often try to be reassuring and even contradict what you say about such a child's retardation, but you don't have to believe them. Parents, when they are well informed, are in an excellent position to interpret retardation to others. You have little right to blame other people for not understanding retardation if you don't give them some help. Others will take cues from your attitudes. Suppose someone tells you that of course your child isn't retarded, or if he is, he'll get over it. If this comes from a casual acquaintance, you can do what you like with it. If it comes from a close relative, you may need and want to put some cards on the table. You may want to say something like "I appreciate your wanting to make us feel better about it, but we have had professional diagnosis and advice and we are willing to work along with the school and our professional advisers. We'd like it if you can accept our information about this child." If you can take this kind of stand, your relatives will probably be more comfortable, and so will you.

Another important point to make to others is that there is no single, right solution to retardation problems. People will tell you, "Did you hear, Mrs. Blank put her child in the state institution — how could she do that?" You know that there isn't any one solution right for all situations, but it seems that everyone else knows there is, only they don't agree on what it is. What is right for one child and one family depends on the child, the rest of the family, the child's behavior, the age relationships, what's available in the community in services, the long-range plans that can be made. You, as parents, of all people, need to be sure of this and to be able to interpret it to others. If someone says to you, "Are you thinking of placing your child in an institution?" you can say a variety of things. "Not at the present time." "Yes, we feel this is best for Dick, although it might not be right for every child." "We haven't decided yet." The point is, you don't have to let other people badger you. You are people of dignity, sense, and courage, who have taken pains to get as full information as possible and when you know what is to be done, you go ahead and do it. But until you are sure what you are going to do, the statement that one answer doesn't work for everyone is a very useful generalization to have at the tip of your tongue.

Close relatives, especially grandparents, are a different problem. Communication with them involves more than just providing information; since inevitably there are emotional overtones, you will need to be understanding but firm. Quite possibly your own parents often can't accept your child's retardation, and cling to the belief that "something will happen," that he will outgrow it. You probably care deeply what they think and want to show them respect. But you simply have to be strong enough and realistic enough to recognize the falsity of their view, and, gradually, to convince them that it is false. Essentially, your behavior has to say, "Look, mother, I'm a big girl now; I don't need to have you lie to me. I know what my child is like." If you can face the facts, perhaps they can. If you can't, or don't, they won't.

Relatives and grandparents sometimes feel that they must "make up" to the handicapped child for being handicapped, and their notion of how to do this is indulgence of his every whim. They give him anything he asks for and some things he didn't think of wishing for. If he does something naughty, they don't punish him — they overlook it and pretend it didn't happen. As a corollary of this, they often pay very little attention to the normal children in the family. Their thinking seems to run along these lines: "There are so many ways in which this retarded child is deprived, and the normal ones get along all right — they have their lives, their friends, their school; they don't need me." We have to keep in mind that older people in our society, whether or not they are grandparents, want to feel needed. Retarded children seem to bring out this feeling in people. But overindulgence by grandparents or other relatives will have harmful effects on a child's behavior, attitude, or both.

Many times, grandparents won't interfere openly. They will maintain an outward attitude of "This is your problem; whatever you decide to do is fine with us." Underneath this statement, though, you may sense some disapproval. You may as a result question whether you're doing the right thing; you may feel let down and wonder, "Why don't they tell me this is right to do? Why don't they say they agree with our planning? Why don't they give us some moral support?" I think if I were the parent of a retarded child, I would object more to silence than to open opposition. You can argue with open criticism, do something about it; passive resistance, as when a grandparent says, doubtfully, "You know best, I suppose," leaves a parent feeling lost. Many grandparents do speak and behave in ways which undermine parents and leave you feeling unsupported, immature, ignorant, wrong. You can't afford to feel that way because these are your decisions, your choices, your problems. Parents need reassurance, support, an expression of confidence in them as people. If a grandparent says, "I know I can't solve this for you; he's your child and you have to do what you think is right, but whatever you decide, I'm behind you 100 percent," this can be an immeasurable boost for the parent of a retarded child.

Grandparents sometimes adopt a teasing or "kidding" approach toward retarded children. This usually results from a feeling of not knowing just how to talk with the child. For example, they might say, "You don't want any ice cream, do you?" A normal child can react to this acceptably; he has some appreciation of teasing fun. But to a retarded child, this may be a confusing, frustrating experience. There may also be a problem with grandparents' temporizing, procrastinating, lying, or making false promises. The retarded child says to his grandmother, "You'll come to my house tomorrow?" She knows perfectly well she isn't coming, but she doesn't want to disappoint him, so she says, "Maybe I can," and he interprets the "maybe" to mean "yes." She probably thinks he'll forget. Probably he won't. Retarded children have to learn to live with disappointments, just as other children do. It would be much better to say in a perfectly sensible fashion, "No, I can't come tomorrow, but I'll see you next week." The uncertainty of the "maybe" is very hard for retarded children.

124

Another thing outsiders and relatives often do is to underestimate the child's level of comprehension in talking about him in his presence. They say, "Oh, isn't it wonderful how much better he is since he's been going to school?" Or, "I understand these children are likely to have special problems when they reach adolescence" — a very good way of suggesting to the pre-adolescent that "anything goes." Comments made in the child's presence can plant in him all kinds of misconceptions and partial understandings, and arouse emotional reactions to the tone of the comment, if not to its content. You can be very direct in handling this problem. Just ask people not to talk about your child in front of him. This is as bad for normal youngsters as for retarded ones.

There are certainly ways in which relatives and grandparents can be of help. Near the top of the list, I would suggest that they be honest. If parents ask for an opinion or for advice, relatives may legitimately give it, but they should do so honestly and openly, without trying to sugar-coat what they say. If they say what they think, when they are asked, this cuts down on the possibility of misunderstanding, which may have emotional consequences. Relatives can sometimes find ways to make it easier for parents to talk with them. Grandparents sometimes say they would like to help, but the child's parents don't seem to want to talk about the situation. Meanwhile, the parents may be saying, "I would like to talk to my parents about our problem, but they don't seem to be interested." The problem may be driving them further apart, when what they would both like is to move closer together. It is especially important for relatives to be able to listen and to refrain from being critical and for parents to be able to accept and talk about the child and his problems.

Relatives can be emotionally supportive and helpful in practical ways. They can invite the retarded child to spend an evening, an afternoon, perhaps even a weekend, with them;

they can plan a special event for him. Any of these is a good way to give parents a little free time. If, however, this arrangement is to succeed, relatives need to check with parents on standards for the child. What are the rules, the limits? How are they enforced? If the retarded child is being entertained jointly with normal brothers or sisters, relatives may need some help on how to differentiate in the handling of the children. What we are seeking here is not perfect consistency, but just some reasonable consistency of rules and expectations. With a retarded child, as with normal children, it is important to keep one's word. If a promise is made it should be kept. This holds for negative as well as positive promises. If punishment is threatened for a misdeed and the child commits the misdeed, he should be punished. Relatives also need to plan some suitable activities for the child. He can go to grandmother's house and behave well for fifteen minutes on Sunday afternoon, but this is a different proposition from going on Saturday afternoon to stay overnight and return home on Sunday afternoon having had no toys or playmates. Grandmother may be willing to read him stories, but he can't be expected to listen to that many stories. Parents can help relatives know what things the child enjoys.

Grandparents and other relatives to be most helpful with a retarded child need to be accepting of him. Accepting him means accepting him the way he is, not trying to make him over into something else. If we are trying to make him over, essentially we are saying, "We don't like you the way you are; stop being the way you are and be the way I want you to be." This is really rejection, although it may be based on good intentions. Letting him be what he is and trying to help him make the most of himself is the kind of acceptance he needs. Relatives, as well as parents, can contribute this quality to the child's life.

13 THINKING ABOUT THE ADOLESCENT YEARS

IN THE literature on mental retardation, there is a shortage of studies and information about adolescent problems of retardates. Perhaps we can make some progress by considering what we know about adolescence in normal youngsters and drawing some comparisons. You may get some help by thinking back to your own feelings and problems as an adolescent, but try not to overgeneralize from these. Times have changed in many ways.

The adolescent period extends from about the age of twelve to the age of nineteen. In some textbooks, adolescence is defined as "a period of storm and stress." Problems of the adolescent period usually arise out of interaction between the child and his family, his age group, and society's standards. Severe adolescent problems in normal teen-agers nearly always involve some contribution by parents. Things do happen, however, in this age range which don't happen before or after. There is rapid physical growth; there are the physical changes involving sexual maturation, with its strong new drives and impulses; there are the psychological components of striving for independence, getting rid of parental authority, and becoming one's own authority. In more primitive societies than ours the spurt in growth and sexual maturation scarcely cause a ripple. Sex is not surrounded by so many cultural taboos and repressive social attitudes. In our society, these still exist despite the changes of recent years.

Children don't all follow exactly the same chronological timetable, but they go through the same stages each at his own pace. The adolescent feels very much concerned about himself. In fact, if you want to draw a parallel, think of the early negativistic stage of the two-year-old who has discovered that he is a separate person and is rebelling against parental authority, and you will find considerable similarity between his behavior and that of the early adolescent. By this time, he has more subtle ways of expressing the "No, I won't" attitude, but the insistence on selfhood and self-determination is similar. If you get annoyed with your adolescents, and you probably do, think how much worse things would be if they didn't reach this stage! You would be saddled with a permanent child.

The young adolescent is fond of thinking long, deep thoughts about himself. Depending on his temperament, this may be a diary-keeping age, an age of close friendships, of self-analysis, or of self-consciousness. Many hours may be spent in front of the mirror, combing hair and putting on makeup, whether it's forbidden or not. Conversation reflects this self-centeredness. Boys may be a little less verbal than girls, but they find their own ways of asserting independence. The age group is important; the young adolescent relies heavily on the weapon that "Everybody else does it." There is conformity in dress, behavior, and language.

Conformity is important partly because the emerging adolescent is so insecure. He seeks security by being like everyone else. At the same time, he is rebelling against his parents, who have for all his life been the ultimate source of authority. He needs a source of strength to lean on while he is rejecting parental control, and the age group furnishes this. Other social changes are going on. He is interested and observant of adult social relationships and becomes more sensitive to the social world of adults. He is probably very idealistic about some causes — which causes will depend, again, partly on his group. He is doing some thinking about his future and what he wants to do with his life, more long-range thinking than he has done before. Adolescents are often more realistic about their abilities than their parents are.

The adolescent is in the difficult position of being between two worlds and not really belonging in either one. He isn't a child any longer, nor is he truly an adult. His parents often increase the ambivalence of his position by their inconsistent demands and comments — "You're too young to date; you're too young for eye makeup," and then in the next breath, "You're old enough to help around here," or "You're too old to act like that."

The young adolescent moves beyond the family frontiers and finds more of his recreation and social life beyond the home and within his age group. Undoubtedly a lot of sexual experimentation goes on; the increase in illegitimacy among teen-agers is evidence of this. It seems apparent that teen-agers often find themselves in situations which they don't know how to handle, with results which are traumatic to personality development and to fulfillment of their potential.

The young adolescent is also likely to be temporarily somewhat emotionally unstable and unpredictable. There are sudden tears, irrational upsets, flareups, and moods. You thought you knew what this child was like, but suddenly he's different. The rapid growth is in itself confusing and a source of insecurity. The child isn't in very good control of his body. The fourteen-year-old boy who can't walk across the kitchen floor without tripping over his feet, which are suddenly size twelve, is embarrassed. Parents say, jokingly, "We can't keep you in shoes." Jokes during this period are apt to be two-edged. I saw an older sister trying to cushion things for a younger brother who literally dropped or spilled everything he picked up by saying, "Cheer up, Billy, in a couple of years you'll be sixteen." He glared at her. Awkwardness is a problem to many youngsters who grow rapidly in a short time. Before they get used to their new size, it has changed again. Many parents and other adults, probably because they also feel awkward, resort to too much teasing or to comments which increase the youngster's self-consciousness. What they ought to talk about is something that takes attention away from the child's growth instead of centering attention on it.

Girls mature physically earlier than boys, by about two years on the average. Because children start school at roughly the same age, this creates another set of social problems. Girls get interested in boys sooner than boys get interested in girls. By the seventh or eighth grade, girls are socially, as well as physically, more mature than boys are. Some youngsters have special problems because of their rate of maturation. The girl who matures early is a misfit for a time. Her interests are changing, but they aren't yet in keeping with her physical maturity. The late-maturing boy is apt not to fit with his group until he catches up. His friends are now interested in girls and dating, and he isn't. Differences in rate of maturation affect adolescents' interest patterns, their own ideas of what it's suitable for them to be doing, and also their friendships. Some children who have been friends all their lives part company when one is an early maturer and one is a late maturer. They seem to pretend that they don't know each other for a while, until the late maturer catches up. Then the friendship may get back on the tracks again.

By middle adolescence, things have calmed down considerably. Once again you find that you can talk with your adolescents. You may be pleasantly surprised at the information they have acquired, at their attitudes, at the depth of their thinking, at their readiness to become adults and to take on responsibility. You have to have accepted the earlier stage of rebellion and relinquished some of the closeness of the parent-child relationship in order to rebuild a different, but equally good, relationship with your older adolescent. This does not mean, however, that you should relinquish authority, or abandon controls, or not provide supervision. You are responsible for maintaining the ground rules, whatever you've decided they are, and holding the line on standards.

When we compare the adolescent period of our retarded children with that of our normal children, there are some differences and some similarities. We see little age difference in physical growth and sexual maturation for most educables and many of the higher ability trainables. For lower ability trainables, there may be more age difference. There seems to be little difference between retarded and normal young adolescents in sexual curiosity and sexual drive. The retarded adolescent may be more naive and less self-protective and "cagey" in his exploratory behavior, and less aware of social taboos. I think that retarded children, like normal children, have some drive for independence, feel some rebellion against parental and other authority. But what the retarded youngster does is influenced by his limited foresight, his relative inability to think about any situation he hasn't experienced, and his relative inability to relate cause and effect. Certainly he has some desire to conform to what the group is doing — if there is a group of which he is part. For youngsters in school, the classroom group is probably their frame of reference. For children not in school, there may not be a group of which he feels a part, so conformity may not be an issue.

The retarded adolescent is not as goal-oriented as the normal adolescent. He is not able to think in long-range fashion about future plans, education, and his choice of job. This doesn't mean that he is unconcerned; he may have considerable anxiety, but this is emotional rather than intellectual. He is anxious, not thoughtful. He may be concerned about a job, but not realistically so. Because of his intellectual defects, the retarded adolescent is less socially aware and less concerned about what's going on in adult social relationships than his normal contemporaries, but this doesn't mean that he has no concern or awareness. His interpretations are limited and often incorrect. He may be observing, but he does not comprehend well what he sees. He may not have a peer group with which to identify; if he doesn't, I would think he might be insecure, since providing security is one of the functions of a peer group. If he feels insecure, I would think he might be inwardly disturbed, although this might not show in outward behavior.

The retarded adolescent is much less likely than normal teen-agers to have many activities outside his home. In general, junior high school parties, church youth group activities, informal evening and after-school socializing, and extracurricular activities are not available for him. If some of an adolescent's energy isn't drained off in such outside activities, it will find expression some other way, perhaps in blowups at home. Or it may be suppressed under a façade of unnatural conformity, of contented immaturity. Parents may not recognize this and may think that they are fortunate to have escaped adolescent problems, when the problems are very much there but in disguised form. Many retarded adolescents, in short, have the same physical maturity, the same sexual drives, and the same adolescent needs, but have fewer suitable outlets. They are likely to be quite frustrated. They also have rapid spurts in growth and less comprehension of what's happening to them. The retardate wants to be like others of his age, but, at some level of understanding or feeling, he knows he isn't.

Many retarded adolescents are out of school programs before they are through being adolescents. At a time when being in a group is vital to them, they may find themselves entirely without a group. For many retarded children, neighborhood contacts decrease in later childhood. By the age of ten, eleven, or twelve, trainable children, who earlier had some good playmates (considerably younger than themselves), often find that no one wants to play with them. For educable children, it may be a year or two later before they find that they aren't well accepted in groups which earlier included them. Some special recreational programs have been set up for retarded adolescents and young adults, and although they probably help, they by no means solve the problem. Often they may have an artificial quality since they aren't an everyday affair, but have to be planned and structured. Usually they are held somewhere that the retarded youngster can't get to by himself, so his parents become involved with transporting him there and picking him up.

Some of the more competent, closer-to-normal educables wage a tremendous battle to be included with normal adolescents; sometimes they almost win. These youngsters eagerly volunteer for things. The normal group perhaps goes so far as to say, "Okay, you can come along," but not "Sure, come along, you're one of us." One may think of this as the tragedy of being "almost" accepted and included. But maybe it isn't always tragic; some of these youngsters may get more reward from being on the outskirts of the normal group than one would think. Perhaps some of them eventually do win more complete acceptance.

Adolescence is a time when parents especially need to be honest about the retardation, especially with the educable group. It has implications for so very many things of concern to adolescents — driving a car, dating, getting married, education, vocational planning. Parents will often need to help the overaspiring adolescent downgrade his vocational goals. You shouldn't wait until your child is an adolescent to do this, but, if you did, you can't wait any longer. Wise parents have been talking realistically to their retarded child for some years about jobs he might like, to help him develop some accepting feelings and attitudes about places in the world of work where he might belong. As he grows older, it is important for him to have a share in making decisions about training and job selection. It must be remembered, however, that he won't have information on which to base a choice; this will have to be provided by school and parents. You need to be careful not to set goals which are too specific because it isn't always possible to know in advance which one might work out for him.

Social skills become important for the older adolescent, especially the educable who is more likely to lead an almost normal community life as an adult. Social courtesies such as knowing when to take your hat off, how to hold a door open for someone else, and how to acknowledge an introduction are taken for granted by many of us, but can be broken down into specific formulas and taught. In general, the more a retarded person can act the way other people act, the more acceptable he will be to other people. Some of the "little things" aren't so little if they spell the difference between seeming like other people or not seeming like them. Appearance is important. People who work with older adolescent retardates report problems of instilling good personal care habits — bathing, neatness, grooming. Parents took care of these things when their child was younger. When he "grew up," they perhaps automatically turned the job over to him without really being aware that he didn't know how to do it. Training in basic habits has to be more specific and continued longer for the retardate than for the normal child. Remember, too, that adolescents, including retardates, at age fourteen or fifteen often reject anything parents try to teach them; it is important to start much earlier.

Sex education and sex information are of concern to parents and with good reason. Nearly everyone agrees that sex education should start in the family at a very early age, not at adolescence. Normally, young children force the issue by asking questions, and parents give some sort of answers to the questions. Parents who refuse to answer or who convey to the child that this isn't "nice" to talk about will force the child to seek information from other sources, which may or may not be factually correct or attitudinally healthy. Because retarded children lack vocabulary and aren't as observant as their normal counterparts, they may not ask questions; but this doesn't mean that they aren't interested in their own bodies or other people's bodies, or that they aren't developing sexual capacities and appetites. In trying to give retarded children some useful sex education, you surely cannot rely on the "birds and the bees." This isn't too much help even for normal children, but for retarded children it is of no help at all. Remember their limited thinking capacity, their inability to generalize. They need straight, simple facts.

Sexual awareness and curiosity do not wait for adolescence. People are biological creatures; sexuality, latent or developed, is a basic part of them. You don't need to be very Freudian in your thinking to see elements of sexual feeling and awareness in much of young children's play. We have tended to deny this in our society, but denial doesn't make it untrue. Little children are curious about sex differences, and preschoolers are likely to do some exploring with each other. When a young child masturbates, parents are often disturbed and tell the child it's "naughty." This has some implications for how we try to manage sex education with retarded children. Marriage is not going to be suitable for many retarded adults because of the family responsibilities it entails. If we are going to rule out marriage for many perhaps we should be careful not to build in too much guilt about masturbation. Perhaps it would be better to make sure that a retardate knows some "where and when" rules. Teach him also not to expose himself in public, not to take his clothes off. It is most important to teach the retarded child to keep his hands off other people. He will surely get into social trouble if he doesn't learn this. In some job-training situations for retardates, it is an ironclad rule not to touch other people.

Retarded children may not ask questions, but this doesn't mean that they shouldn't receive information. When there are other children in the family, it is easier to present facts about sex because the other children are asking questions. If you don't have other children, or they are much older, you don't have this natural teaching situation. Much of what we include in sex education is really terminology and vocabulary. Many of our more severely retarded children will be, at some point in their lives, living in institutions or at least not with their parents. Teaching children proper vocabulary for parts of the body is important not only for attitudes but for communication. They may need to be able to tell somebody where they hurt. If they don't know words to use, communication will be difficult.

Whatever you do about sex education will be determined within your own family by how you feel about it, but do think about it, as objectively as you can. As you plan for your own children, keep in mind that anything surprising, unexpected, and not understood can be traumatic to a child, and feeling guilty is part of the trauma. Consider the girl who isn't prepared for her first menstrual period. Her first reaction is that she is wounded; she may well be frightened and try to conceal the evidence. This suggests that she feels guilty. Advance preparation is one way to avoid the guilt feeling. (I think many retarded children feel some guilt because they are retarded. This is an emotional rather than an intellectual reaction. They can't describe it or explain it, but they feel they did something wrong to deserve this.)

Some parents say, "I'm willing to tell my child about sex, but he won't understand it anyway." True enough. Your normal three-year-old doesn't comprehend it either. Even your normal twelve-year-old doesn't understand it completely. Whether the retarded child understands or not is less important than the feeling he gets of not being shut out.

We can formulate some general principles for parents. One is that parents should be careful to avoid setting marriage as an inevitable goal for a retarded child. Many higher ability retardates will marry and lead nearly independent lives, but when they are children, it is difficult to predict in advance for which ones marriage will be suitable. Most trainables should not be allowed to marry at all. As parents, long before this becomes an issue, you can encourage your retarded child to think along other lines. When your retarded daughter says she is going to get married and have four children, instead of agreeing with her, you can say, "Well, some people get married, but not everyone. Maybe you won't want to get married." One of the risks of marriage for the retarded, whether the retardation is inheritable or not, is the probability that they cannot be good parents, for it is unlikely that they will be able to provide adequate guidance for children, whatever the ability level of the children. It may be more tragic for a normal or bright child to have a retarded parent than for a retarded child to have a retarded parent.

Earlier in this century, many states passed laws authorizing sterilization for retarded persons. In some states, sterilization was compulsory; in others, permissive, requiring the consent not only of the retarded person but also of his nearest relatives — parents or spouse. As views on the causation of retardation changed, with many causes other than genetic ones discovered and better understood, sterilization was less often used. Then, too, as more efforts were made to keep retarded people within the framework of the normal society rather than institutionalized, arguments about their civil rights had an import on public thinking. Abstract arguments by those without direct experience with retardates should not, however, blind us to the facts. A retarded adult may be capable of functioning in society on a limited basis, perhaps able to earn a living, and be reasonably self-sufficient. For higher ability retardates, marriage can be a very stabilizing influence. It provides companionship, love, and security. But introduce the responsibilities of reproduction and the "marginally sufficient" individual is likely to sink into dependence. Among parents I have talked with there is an increasing conviction that in many cases sterilization, both for retarded girls and for retarded boys, is a protection that parents should provide. Social attitudes in general may not yet accept this, but many parents of retarded children, adolescents, and young adults seem convinced of the wisdom of this course of action. Some medical doctors assert that complete hysterectomies are desirable for retarded girls who are not able to cope with the self-care involved in the menstrual process, and for whom this constitutes a special dependency during many years of their lives.

Whatever parents decide about sterilization, the need for supervision of retardates continues and becomes more difficult in adolescence. When the adolescent becomes sexually interested his parents may react by imposing more supervision and tighter control. This may lead to anger, resentment, and rebellion, or it may result in continuance of dependency which in other ways the child doesn't need and should be outgrowing. Too close supervision may mean that he can have fewer social contacts and must spend more time alone; this can lead to personality and adjustment problems. But we do need to know where the retarded adolescent is, whom he is with, and what he is doing. We don't want our retardates to exploit other people, nor do we want them to be exploited by others. Achieving a proper balance is no easy matter.

When children of nursery school age are physically curious about each other, adults aren't too concerned. Retarded children reach adolescence with mental ages of four, five, and six, and show this same preschool type of curiosity. What was easy to accept in the four-year-old is hard to accept in the fourteen-year-old, even though the mental maturity level is the same. The physical maturity level is very different and sexual impulses are also different. This is one reason for the loss of neighborhood playmates as the trainable child grows older. People are uncomfortable when the fourteen-year-old adolescent retarded boy is playing with five-year-olds. He may not be doing anything at all wrong, but people are concerned about the possibility and with some just reason. Four-year-old thinking combined with fourteen-year-old behavior is different from four-year-old behavior across the board. One possibly useful approach has already been mentioned: stressing "hands off." Teach retarded children, from childhood on, not to touch playmates and not to let anyone touch them, and also not to go anywhere with a stranger. This sounds rather old-fashioned, but if we want to protect retardates from exploitation, it might be helpful.

In deciding how to handle the awakening sexual interest of the retarded adolescent, parents should take into consideration what the expectations are for the retardate's future. Do we anticipate that he will be employable and will lead a fairly normal life? If so, we want to give him basic information in sex education and try to instill in him good attitudes toward interpersonal relationships and love relationships. We would plan differently for a retardate of a 40 IQ who might have a job in a sheltered workshop but who would remain in the community either in the home of his parents or in a boarding home, and would not be responsible for managing his own life. For most trainables, we think of semi-dependence; for most educables, we can think more of semi-independence. But ability is not the only trait to be considered; other aspects of behavior also must be taken into account. Is he aggressive, curious, active? What we know of personality development suggests that the more active, exploratory child will also be more active and exploratory in sex behavior. It is important to keep in mind too the overlap between sexual impulses and physical drives and the affectional and security needs people have. Often what appears as sex behavior represents an attempt to find attention, affection, security, and approval. We need to look for other satisfactions for the retardate in these important areas of personal security.

There are few answers. No one has given us very good road maps to help our retardates learn about sex, needed controls, or suitable outlets. One helpful point to remember is that habit formation for retarded people is extremely important. If good habits can be inculcated, the retardate is likely to continue to follow the path which has been established.

14 PLANNING FOR THE FUTURE

It is difficult and often painful for parents of retarded children to look into the future. While retardates are still children, it is easy to view them as being younger than their ages because behaviorally and intellectually they are — but they do grow up. And it is essential that parents plan for their future. Unlike normal children who themselves do much of their own planning, retarded children must rely largely on their parents.

Many factors are involved in planning for retarded children. A logical place to start is with the degree of the child's retardation. Being grown-up involves competing with other people for one's share of material things. The more retarded the individual, the more disadvantaged he is in this competition. How independent he can be, to what extent he can earn his living and make his own decisions, are partly determined by intelligence level — but only partly. They are also determined by personality traits, by other handicaps, and by the goals and values he has learned as a member of his family. Sometimes we stop there in describing what determines a retardate's future and forget a very important factor — that of circumstance, situation, "good luck." Whether or not an individual can get a job depends partly on whether there is a job available. The circumstances in which the person lives

141

help determine how successfully and how independently he can live. Circumstances change with time and place. We used to think that a farm was an ideal place for a retarded person because there he had less social competition, and there were more things he could do, or at least help to do, and there was built-in supervision because someone else was always around. But farming has changed; it has become more complex, more scientific, and more highly mechanized. Today other situations may be better for the retardate.

We can use the evidence of the past to guide us in planning for the adulthood of retarded children. There have been many follow-up studies of retarded children carried out in different parts of the country over the past fifty years. Some studies which were published in the 1920's have almost the same things to say as some published in the 1960's, and those done in Lincoln, Nebraska, have results similar to those done in Boston, Massachusetts, or Minneapolis, Minnesota. Many of the findings are remarkably consistent. Most studies found that from two-thirds to four-fifths of educable youngsters studied at later ages were at least marginally self-sufficient as adults. The age of the group at the time of the follow-up is significant. If the group was at an average age of twenty-five when studied, fewer of the retardates were in the self-sufficient category than if the average age at the time of the study was forty-five. In interpreting this finding, we have to consider the national economic picture at the time of the study. If the study done when the group was twenty-five coincided with the depths of the depression, circumstances were against the retarded. If the follow-up of forty-five-year-olds coincides with a better economic climate, then circumstances were more favorable for them. The influence of circumstances is probably not the only factor, however. There may be some maturational and habit-formation factors operating which help the retarded to settle down and operate in a routine, so that with experiences of relative success, they will make a better adjustment if these experiences continue over a longer time span.

While we are thinking about the proportion of retardates who can achieve economic self-sufficiency, it is well to keep in mind the normal curve of distribution. There are more retarded with IQs between 70 and 80 than there are with IQs between 60 and 70, so we can assume, with good probability of being right, that more of the self-sufficient group of retardates fall in the higher ability range. The studies do show, however, that intelligence level is not the only pertinent factor. Some retardates found to be self-sufficient were at the lower end of the educable group. It is difficult for studies to evaluate other influences in the person's life. What kinds of family supervision and aid were available? What kind of emotional support? Who helped him make decisions? Whom did he marry? The follow-up studies found that retarded girls often married "upward" in intelligence range, which may have some disadvantages but probably has some economic advantages. If your daughter with a 65 IQ marries a nice boy of average ability, her chances of leading a socially adequate life are probably better than if she married a nice boy at her own ability level. Retarded boys, on the other hand, aren't as socially mobile as the girls; they more often marry girls within their own IQ range, so matrimony is less likely to "rescue" them.

It must also be remembered that this higher ability group, in the 70 to 80 IQ range, by and large includes more of those whose retardation was not caused by something specifically "knowable." It was more likely caused by some chance hereditary factors operating. This group, in general, has been found to be more adaptable and more absorbable in society than some of the children in whom there has been brain damage, seizure problems, and organic malfunctions.

The follow-up studies describe the personality traits which

are of crucial importance in adult adjustment and adequacy: good attitudes toward other people, ability to follow directions, willingness to do what is asked, cooperation, dependability, responsibility, thoroughness, and being able to do a job. The general quality of stability (not getting into trouble) is important, as is the ability to handle money adequately, and not get into debt. Simple likability as a person is another asset. Some people are more likable than others. People, in general, respond somewhat negatively to traits which both normal and retarded individuals may have: We don't like people who are conceited or self-centered, or who lie, cheat, or steal, or who can't be depended on, or who lose their tempers or get their feelings hurt too easily; we generally don't like people who are unkind to others or are too suspicious or have a chip on their shoulder. All these traits, to some degree, may be found in nearly everyone, but we react to the pattern. With retarded adults, some of these traits constitute additional handicaps, and they don't have enough assets in their personality bank to balance them. Normal people often do.

We can expect, then, that for educable children with IQs above 60 who do not have other severe problems, physical or emotional, the chances are about three out of four that they can be marginally self-sufficient or better — depending on training, environment, circumstances, and luck. For educable children with an IQ below 60, the chances of self-sufficiency are probably less on the average, but we can expect that these chances will also be influenced by personality and behavior traits.

There are, as already suggested, situational factors that will affect the chances of retardates. Social conditions and job opportunities change over time. Automation introduces changes; military service requirements shift from time to time. Methods of training and education also change. Attitudes change. All these things influence opportunities for the retarded.

In any event parents will often need to be persistent and well-motivated to explore resources for prevocational and vocational training that may be available for their educable child within their own community or state. The first area to explore is what is available within the public school system. Not too long ago, special education often terminated when the child reached age sixteen; usually, this coincided with the end of the elementary school program of special education. Gradually, provisions within the school system have expanded for both the junior high school and the senior high school age range, in directions which include extended, modified academic programs—nonacademic or less academic subject matter, prevocational training, work-school combination programs, and training in vocational skills. Often state vocational rehabilitation programs are coordinated with school programs. For post-school youngsters, state vocational rehabilitation services may offer a variety of services, including job training, attention to medical and sensory handicaps, and sometimes state-sponsored sheltered-work situations for periods of training. In addition to seeking out what the school system has to offer, and what vocational rehabilitation programs have to offer at the state, regional, and local levels, parents may get information through their state or local Association for Retarded Children.

For most trainable ability youngsters, the job situation is less hopeful than for educables. The ultimate potential of trainables is not great enough for competitive employment or for day-to-day independence in living. We have to think of the trainable adult as a person who will be semi-dependent throughout his lifetime. He may be able to do useful work — at home, in a sheltered workshop, in a sympathetic small group situation, or in an institutional setting—provided he is carefully taught to do it and is under fairly constant supervision. Not all trainables will be able to do this; as with educables, how successful they will be vocationally will depend partly on their other traits. A trainable may, or may not, be able to have friends, companionship, and suitable off-the-job activities. This will depend partly on where he is and on what is available. He may, or may not, need constant supervision. This will depend partly on his behavior traits, and not just on his ability level.

Clearly in our society at the present time the possibilities for trainable adults are very limited. A trainable youngster may stay at home as long as his parents can take care of him and supervise him. This may continue into adulthood, but by the nature of the life process, it cannot go on forever. The life span of the trainable retarded is longer than it used to be. Many of them — perhaps most of them now — will outlive their parents. If we rely on family responsibility, we probably come to the end of the road at the death of the parents. Sometimes, brothers and sisters are expected to take over at this point, but this is usually unfair and unjust. By this time, it is not only the brother or sister who is involved, but his whole family. Whether or not the adult retardate can stay at home, with parents or other family, without too much difficulty, depends on his temperament and disposition, as well as on what is available for him to do. Some trainables are too restless. Some develop emotional problems and behavior problems in adolescent years in spite of the best situation parents have been able to provide. Often parents ask, "What did we do wrong?" The answer is often "Nothing," specifically, except perhaps the child was kept in a situation where his satisfactions were too few and his frustrations too many until a blowup finally came.

There are some partial solutions on the horizon. We are seeing the development of living facilities — large boarding homes or small residential institutions — which can provide round-the-clock supervision, some recreational programs, and companionship. Some of these also offer sheltered-workshop employment or low-level job training. Some provide a living arrangement for retarded adults who can hold a job but need a place to live. For the local situation, the county welfare department is in a good position to provide information and advice, as is the Association for Retarded Children. Availability of some financial help, through Aid to the Disabled programs and through Social Security, should be explored by parents.

Public school programs are now giving more attention to the lower ability retardate at the low-educable and high-trainable levels. Many of these programs are built around concrete learning, development of good work habits and attitudes, and cultivation of favorable personality adjustments. These will not make all retardates employable, but, over time, they will help sort out those in whom the essential traits of employability can be culturated.

At the present time, states are working toward decreasing their institutional populations and making better use of expanded local facilities. It seems clear, however, that there will always be a need for some state-supported residential facilities to provide care, supervision, and training. Very often, for the trainable-ability adult who cannot achieve a meaningful life in the community, a good institution should be the first choice of plan.

Residential institutions offer some real benefits for many retardates. Almost always retardates relax and show fewer behavior disturbances; the competition is decreased; they are out from under pressure. They have a very steadying kind of routine, fewer adjustments to make, and a simplified life. If we try to think about what living in the normal world might feel like for a retardate, this makes some sense. We may simplify demands on the retardate, but we cannot always simplify the total world.

147

It is hard for parents to look ahead for their retarded child because his very characteristics keep belying his age. You live with him; you know you can't treat him like a ten-year-old, so you don't try to, and you forget that he is ten. Chronological time goes on, whether mental development does or not. He behaves at a younger age, reinforcing your perception of him as being younger than he is. The older he grows, the more he falls behind what is expected of his age. But it is hard to keep his limitations in mind. You get used to living with a retarded child. You forget what you expected of your normal child.

Planning for the future is, of course, a process which has to be individualized. It is primarily the parents' responsibility to make decisions, but it is the role of the school and of other social agencies to be more objective, more realistic, and more honest — to ask themselves the questions that need to be answered honestly, realistically, objectively before decisions can be made. What can the retardate do that demands little abstract intelligence? It may be something that takes motor skill, and degrees of motor skill differ among those at the same general ability level. What other handicaps does he have — health problems, seizure problems, speech problems, stamina, sensory defects? How good are his social adjustment and habits of reacting to others? How does he get along with others of his own age and with people in authority? What are his attitudes toward rules and punishment? What kind of disposition does he have — how easily does he get angry, and how does he show his anger? Is it more directed at people or at things? Is it violent, uncontrolled, or just an outlet? How much control does he have? How does he feel about work? Does he enjoy being busy and feeling useful? Does he use caution? Does he recognize dangers? These are observations parents can make that will be useful in planning.

It is essential to begin making these observations at the elementary school age level. Think about what your child is like now, and what things about him worry you. You may tell yourself, "He'll outgrow that," but what if he doesn't? Don't try to sugar-coat the things that worry you. Keep them in mind, along with the things that please and reward you. Don't shut the evidence of the child's behavior out of your thinking. Consider where he could fit in later on if he is still pretty much the way he is now. Consider how much society can adapt. To what extent can we expect that neighbors, relatives, storekeepers, employers, bus drivers, salespeople will want to make allowances, or know what allowances to make?

In the decision-making process, look too at what the child is getting out of living. When he is small, it is easy to pretend that he is an extension of you. The longer he lives, the less you can pretend this, and the less it is true. He is his own person. What satisfactions, interests, companionship, and activities are available to him? Your normal children move away from you in independence and choice-making; you react to this by modifying your own behavior and letting them go. Someone has said that the major task of a parent is to stop being one. When our retarded adolescents and young adults try to move toward independence and self-determination, we are likely to be more upset — yet they, too, have a feeling of selfhood. We can't know exactly how they feel because they can't explain it to us, but we can see it in their behavior. They are themselves and we cannot live their lives for them, but we can, and must, think wisely about where and how they can best live their own lives.

15 UNDERSTANDING OURSELVES BETTER

IN THE preceding chapters the focus has been on the retardate — how he came to be that way, what his special problems are, what approaches can be used to help him develop to the fullest of his potential, what planning needs to be done for him. Now let us look at you who are parents. To your children, normal, gifted, or retarded, you are the most important people in the world. How well you fulfill your responsibilities to them — and to yourselves — depends in a large part on your own emotional self-adjustment.

At the core of adult adjustment, in my viewpoint, is a sense of self-value. This is partly self-respect, but more than self-respect. It's a feeling of being worth something to yourself, to your family, to the world, but first of all to yourself. If you don't have this, you may be in trouble. This problem is at the root of many of the emotional disturbances people have. Where did it come from? Much of it came from our childhood. Did our parents help us feel we were valuable as people? Did they care about us, not because of what we did, but because of what we were? We've already seen how this operates with retarded children: as personalities, they are likely to develop in desirable ways when they feel valued, not for what they do but for who they are, because they are themselves. This is equally true for normal people.

There are times for all of us when our self-value is challenged. Then we are likely to use what are called by psychologists "defense mechanisms." We might compare them to the safety valves of the pressure cooker. It is important to recognize that these are not always bad. We all have them and need them. They become bad only when they get out of balance, when they run away with us, when the safety valve doesn't close and all the steam — our energy — escapes. The better we understand them, the more they can become useful tools for us.

Rationalization is a common defense mechanism. So we say we were late for the meeting because traffic was heavy, and we don't mention that we didn't leave until half an hour after we should have left. That would reflect on us, whereas to say that the traffic was heavy reflects on circumstances beyond our control. We say of one of our children, "He had a terrible time in the second grade; he had the worst teacher you've ever seen." Well, maybe he did; maybe he didn't. Even if it's true, it is not necessarily the whole truth. What it amounts to is that for us this may be the most acceptable reason. Rationalization is so common that probably not half an hour passes in most of our lives that we don't, either out loud or to ourselves, make some use of this device. It is a handy way not only to protect ourselves from other people, but also to protect ourselves from ourselves. It's all right to tell yourself a good lie now and then — provided that part of you still knows what you're doing. There are people who tell themselves such good "reasons" that they hardly know the truth when they meet it face to face. This is a dangerous habit because we need to hang onto the ability to discriminate.

Denial and repression are more complicated. Something happens that we don't like, so we say it didn't happen. This is a difficult position to maintain because it is an outright falsehood; it isn't just a round-the-barn excuse like a rationalization. If something happens, and you say it didn't, you are denying reality. You can't get away with that very well; it is too clear to you. So the next thing you tend to do is to change reality to fit your interpretation, and you do this by conveniently burying the things that you can't tolerate or escape. You drive them down into your underneath layers of thought, like driving a nail into a piece of wood. Repression banishes something you can't tolerate into an unaware part of you, so you don't have to tolerate it. You deny to some degree that it exists. To say, "I won't worry about that, I'll forget about it for now," is all right if you do come back to look at the problem later. Or to forget something unpleasant that you can't do anything about, if you really can't do anything about it, may save you unnecessary pain. If you have a retarded child, this is a fact that won't go away no matter how much you deny it. Put out of your mind your embarrassment at the unfortunate scene your retarded child made in the restaurant when he thought the waiter was taking away what was his; but acknowledge to yourself that because he is retarded you will have to make sure he understands restaurant procedures before you take him again. However, there are potential dangers in repression. You start denying one thing, and this leads to denying something else. Such distorting of reality, if it becomes a habit, is not healthy. The worst of it is that the more you do it, the less you know you're doing it, and the less you know you're doing it, the less you can stop it. Good friends and good professional help can come to your rescue; but it's better not to let yourself fall into the habit of repressing things that bother you.

Compensation is a relatively healthy device. You have a shortcoming in some skill, so you try to make up for it by developing some other skill. An extreme example of this is the crippled child who would like to play baseball but can't so he becomes a sports writer or a radio broadcaster. Another example would be the mother of the retarded child who, frustrated because she cannot make him over, devotes her energies to programs for groups of retarded children — committees, parent association work, benefits.

People use other defense mechanisms. They run away — not always physically, but they seek escape in various ways, some of which are good, some less good, some risky, some downright dangerous. Acceptable escapes are going to movies, reading detective stories, watching television, daydreaming — if it doesn't take you too far afield or you don't do it when you really ought to be working. Alcohol is risky — a very good escape for some people, but a very poor solution to whatever they're escaping from. It's true that if you get mildly intoxicated, you can forget your troubles; if you do this habitually enough, you'll forget other things too — that you're a person with things to live for and achievements to strive for. People don't always recognize sleep as a form of escape. This sounds innocent enough — you're tired, so you take naps, go to bed early, sleep late. The sleep needs of people do differ, but some people sleep a lot because they don't want to live their life the way it is.

Projection is a device responsible for much social difficulty. We don't like to blame ourselves, so we blame other people. If we work at it hard enough and reinterpret the facts with enough determination, we can be fairly convincing to ourselves. An interesting thing about projection is that we tend to be critical of other people for the things we don't like to admit in ourselves. The next time you find yourself saying something negative about someone, no matter who it is, just stop and look at the traits you're criticizing, and then take a look at yourself. The chances are good that you will find some reason why you're so sensitive to this behavior in the other person. You don't really like the trait in yourself, but it is too threatening to admit this. So you say instead, "Isn't he impossible?" and you get it off your back, onto someone else's. We do many things with projection. We become suspicious of people, and feel that they are being critical of us. It's really we who are being critical of them, but we can't face this, so we reverse it and say "they" are being critical of us. In an extreme form, we find this characteristic in severely disturbed people. In a mild form, we find it in most people. Some of this often has roots in early childhood and is related to punishment and things we felt guilty about.

We may use physical symptoms such as headaches, backaches, stomachaches, and leg aches as an excuse for not doing something we don't want to do or as a way to turn attention away from something we don't want noticed. This begins early in many children and is often fostered by parents who are concerned about their child and focus on health — sometimes with reason, when a child has had a lot of illness, sometimes not. Children pick up this pattern early. I suspect that people who learn early to express anxiety through physical symptoms are likely to continue in this pattern. It isn't always disabling. Some people insist on working harder than ever when they are sick, as though to say, "I'm in terrible shape, but I'm a martyr. For heaven's sake, please notice how awful I feel and how hard I'm working and what a martyr I am. If you don't notice, the game is over." All of us have some of this trait, too. If we make a special effort when we don't feel good, we want someone to notice it.

All these things are part of people. As parents of retarded children, you have had strong challenges to your feeling of self-value. You've been overloaded with guilt, anxiety, concern, worry, conflict, ambivalence, confusion, and depression. The special problems you've faced may have accentuated your need to use some of the self-defensive devices. Some of these devices we can laugh about, especially in others; we should be aware of all of them and be willing to think about them if we are seeking ways to find more maturity, more balance, more health and steadiness in ourselves. I am convinced that not only can people continue to grow up emotionally after they are grown up in years, but they can do much of this through their own efforts, self-awareness, and thoughtfulness. I'm not talking about self-psychotherapy, but only about applying thought and common sense to viewing one's own life.

How can you help yourself emotionally? An important starting point is not to kid yourself. Some people seem to be gifted with more insight than others. Even so, there is nothing to prevent our practicing looking at ourselves and trying to see what really underlies what we are doing. Look at the reasons why you do some things and avoid doing others, and then look at the reasons you tell yourself, and see if they match. If they don't there's some self-deception going on. What excuses do you make for not doing the things you don't do? What excuses do you make to yourself for attitudes you have which you really don't like to see in yourself and don't want to accept as part of you? What rationalizations do you make about them? Look at the things you say when you are just chattering along to yourself about yourself in day-to-day living. When you are criticized for something, subtly or not so subtly, a natural reaction is to strike back with a "So are you" reaction, and not listen any further. It's natural, but immature. When you find yourself reacting like this, take another look. Consider the criticism, and question yourself about it. Ponder a bit — "Was it correct, maybe? Did I get mad because it's a little too true for comfort?" Nobody likes to be criticized, but we sometimes reject criticism when we ought to think about it and take account of some part of it. Sometimes we would like to be different, but we are inwardly afraid that we might not be able to change so we pretend we don't want to change.

You can practice accepting yourselves. Many parents of retarded children are very self-derogatory, taking on themselves blame for things which they couldn't possibly have helped. What may have happened in this parent-child situation is that, having a child who is hard to value in the conventional ways, you substitute valuing him in place of valuing yourself. In a way, you sell yourself down the river to give the child a place in the sun. Should you, or shouldn't you? I don't know. I do know, however, that for the individual parent, this is not a healthy thing to do. It does not take you to more constructive ways of behaving.

You can avoid being too conscientious, having too high standards. Perfectionism can keep you so busy twenty-four hours a day you won't have time to make long-range decisions; you're too busy turning corners of the sheet at just this angle and putting the dishes on the shelf at just that angle. Having high expectations of yourself may seem like a moral, noble trait, but carried to extremes, it won't make you an easy person to live with and won't lead to constructive solutions to problems. You may also be led to be critical of other people, which helps you think highly of yourself. If you can be accepting of yourself and not create artificial standards, you can also be more accepting of other people and not need to be so critical of them. Then you'll be more comfortable both with yourself and with others. This sounds simple, but that doesn't mean it's easy to do. People do have different standards, values, and ways of living; remember that they also have different problems.

One secret of a good emotional climate is acceptance of individual differences. This is often a key to the comfortableness of a good situation for working, teaching, or living. Acceptance is nebulous to talk about or try to define, but it is not hard to recognize when you see it in action. If you try to think of the two or three people with whom you are the most comfortable, chances are you will find that they are people who do accept individual differences.

With other people, we have to expect some problems in social interaction. People in organizations and on committees often get into conflicts not because they're all trying to do a job and see different ways to do it, but because they're all trying to do a job and see different ways to defend their own personalities, which can lead to supercriticalness. How do you handle this kind of controversy when you meet it in, say, a parent-teacher organization? One thing that helps is to anticipate the problems; then we won't be as disturbed when they happen. Another is to cultivate skill in communication. Much interpersonal difficulty is a failure of words which happens because people have different experiences with words, so they mean different things to different people. One way to avoid this is not to talk in the longest words you know, but in the shortest. Reduce things as far as possible to what is concrete, what is visible and touchable. When we communicate, both professionally and nonprofessionally, we sometimes mistake the word for the fact and forget that the word does not mean the same fact to someone else. This poses some problems, of course. The minute we become concrete, realistic, and factual, we run the risk of hurting people's feelings. We may have to balance the importance of good communication, and the long-range purposes it can serve, against the risk of hurting feelings.

Most of us live with some double standards; there are differences between what we say and what we know. A little boy hits his brother, and we say, "Don't hit your brother — you love your brother." He says, "No, I don't; I hate him." Then we say, "Of course you don't hate him; he's your brother; you love him." This is part of the double standard. We say feelings are positive, nice, good; we often try to deny the negative ones — fear, hate, anger, hostility, aggressiveness — and pretend that these feelings are not part of us. Of course they are; the negative and positive feelings are both there; that's just the way people are put together. When we deny the reality and the existence of the negative feelings we are creating some psychological problems.

Talking about problems and getting explanations doesn't always have to threaten people. You can ask, "Why do you want to do it that way?" This doesn't criticize the way; it only says, "I don't understand your point of view." The risk of hurting people is also diminished by keeping our attention on the goal, the process, the activity, and the purpose, rather than on the people involved; this means learning to use a problem-solving attitude, a "What can be done here?" approach.

In interpersonal conflict, someone must take the initiative to reestablish communication; someone must say, "Let's talk about it." Many problems would yield to this honest attack. Often we are afraid to take action because we aren't sure it is the right action, but even a wrong action can sometimes clarify a situation and the factors at work. If everyone stands around doing nothing, or goes home in a sulk, not only does the problem remain unsolved, but we even fail to define what the problem is. If we take some action, even if it's wrong, we may find out that it's wrong and do something different. If it's right, the problem is moved closer to solution.

It's good for people to use their energies constructively. It's good to identify with other people and projects; this is part of getting into motion. You can see yourself better, see other people better, and view your problems more clearly. You may even see a place to attack them. Activity is important in people's adjustment. At the same time, you don't have to do things that put you under tension if they are not essential in meeting your responsibilities. Living with a retarded child creates severe strains. You are often jittery, nervous; you may not be able to sleep. If certain activities make things worse, even if you feel that you "ought" to do them, don't! Relieve strain where you can and don't feel that you are babying yourself.

Say "No" to some requests; take it a little easier. Seek some ways of satisfying your own desires; do things you have long wanted to do but put aside because of competing pressures. This is part of maintaining a sense of self-value. If there are things that would make you feel a more "comfortable with you" person, you should try to revise your life to include some of these, and not feel that you are sacrificing your child if you do.

The important thing is to give your child a set of parents who are complete and healthy people. It isn't fair to anyone in the family when parents decide that they are too busy with their retarded child to take time for any other satisfactions in living. Being unfair to yourselves does not create any more fairness for your retarded child, and may, in fact, deprive him of the good "parenting" you could otherwise be giving him.

Index

DATE DUE

DEC 1 8 1975		
FEB 1 1977		
MAY 1 9 1977		
SE 29 '81		
OC 20 '81		
AP 19 '87		
DEC 10 EC 1 0 1991		
NOV 1 8 1992		
GAYLORD		PRINTED IN U.S.A